MW01298106

The New Millennium NoteBooks
Windows on the Past
Volume 1 – Part 1

The Universe – A Realistic Look at Our Beginnings
Rewriting Mankind's Cosmic History

Norma Hickox

The Universe – A Realistic Look at Our Beginnings
A Chrysalis Publication

ISBN-13: 978-1986820721

Published by Chrysalis Publications 20168
email: nhickox@gmail.com
www.chrysalispub.com

Photography and graphics by Neil Hickox
Cover photo – The Horsehead Nebula (NASA)

Norma - My Story
by
Norma Hickox

Are You Curious About Channeling?

FREE digital book about channeling by Norma Hickox.

•Ever wonder if you could do it, or if you should do it?

•Norma has been channeling for 35 years and has published twelve books of insights.

- Learn how it all started with her and why she continued to do it.
- Her mission, so to speak, is to tie science and spirituality together.
- She has had teachings sent through by such beings as Joseph (father of Jesus), Ezekiel, Tesla, Jesus, Michael (the Creator God), and many others.

Go to www.chrysalispub.com for details on how to get this free book.

PREFACE

The New Millennium NoteBooks, based on The Chrysalis Teachings, will benefit those seeking to become better people by allowing them to ponder the fact that they are not alone in this universe; that there is structure to their path and definite goals ahead to continually strive for.

I believe that these teachings will allow people to finally understand their dual nature; that without allowing the growth of the soul to take place they are not much higher on the evolutionary pole than the animals. Someday the animals will evolve to the same stage as a human who is not expressing the soul. When people begin to understand this, they will begin to look at life differently and will be more willing to stay on the spiritual path of progress

The New Millennium NoteBooks are roadmaps for growth – physically, emotionally, mentally and spiritually, and serve to educate and explain much that remains a mystery. I believe that if people could get a big picture of where they came from and how they developed, it would serve them well in their interactions with each other and help promote peace in the world.

These notebooks cover a wide range of topics encompassing all spiritual disciplines. They are divided into three sections, "Windows on the Past," "Journeys in the Present" and "Pathways to the Future."

Windows on the Past

FROM THE AUTHOR

I am a professional musician. I play and teach six instruments and compose music. I have been an organist and choir director for many different spiritual denominations and have also taught vocal music in private elementary and pre-schools. In the past I played in the pit orchestra for a musical theater group and also in a dance band, eventually having my own dance band. I have played numerous solo appearances, some on TV and played a Christmas Eve church service for former President Ford and his family in Vail, Colorado. Along with music, my career has also included involvement with the arts of painting, writing, dance and theater that led to my writing two musical plays with original music.

I live with my son Neil and his family, wife Claudia, daughter Fiorella and son Leland in Simi Valley, California. Neil did the artwork for all of the New Millennium Notebooks. He is a computer scientist and amateur photographer. Without his help not only for the artwork, but also in keeping my computer operating properly, these books probably would not have come into being.

I've been blessed with the privilege or gift of "knowing" many spiritual truths. It seems that some part of my makeup has the ability to "know" and "see" into different time periods of the past. I call this higher aspect of my soul the "TimeTraveler." Actually being a musician, it was the vibrations of music that I've been exposed to since the age of four that enables me to have this insight. The TimeTraveler is the transformer of the vibrations and the interpreter of higher plane information on which I rely to understand the thought pictures I access.

The TimeTraveler

The TimeTraveler rides on his magic carpet of time powered by the vibration of the colors of the rainbow which match the vibrations of the musical scale of C. The TimeTraveler himself vibrates at the tone of "middle C." He has the ability to travel instantly to any time period of the universe. A small picture of him will appear at the beginning of the material given by the TimeTraveler for each chapter.

I hope you will allow yourself to imagine that perhaps I have been given incredible insight into some of the mysteries of the universe. Please allow your mind to expand and wonder "what if" it all took place as shown to me.

These teachings will clearly show that
Birth (Creation) and Development (Evolution)
go hand in hand. You cannot have one without the other.

Harmony in the Universe
Poem by Norma

In the vastness of space
And in the stillness of time
There is a Harmony
Causing the stars to shine.

Each star on its own
Would look black in space
But there is a Harmony
That lights up each one's face.

The vastness of the universe
Seems so huge and strange
But there is a Harmony
That round about does range.

There is no wind as such
No sound of anything
But there is a Harmony
That makes it seem to sing.

All around we sense our God
In all His many forms
Be glad there is a Harmony
That brings Him to our arms.

If all were truly still
And all were truly dark
Then we'd have no Harmony

Naught would leave a mark.

When looking at the heavens
And sending thoughts to God
Be sure to feel this Harmony
Tis' the way we all must trod.

Harmony is God, my friend
In everything we do
This Harmony is God, so
Let the Harmony be you.

TABLE OF CONTENTS

Chapter One

THE BIRTH OF OUR UNIVERSE

From high up on Mt. Evans in Colorado my son Neil had his tripod sat up to take pictures. He was on vacation from his home in California and had wanted to get in some picture taking. It had clouded up and suddenly it was raining. We made a mad dash for the car. After the storm had passed, we were treated to a beautiful rainbow. We were actually above the rainbow looking down on it.

Rainbow, Mt. Evans, Colorado

"Rainbows are one of the most marvelous things in nature," I said to Neil. "I believe they were given to us to allow our mind to travel beyond everyday thinking. How can anyone look at a rainbow and not wonder where you would arrive if you could literally get on the rainbow and travel its path?"

"Yeah," said Neil, "Do you remember the double one we saw in the canyon behind our house?"

"I sure do," I replied, "and how about the upside down rainbow we saw in Nevada after Mt. St. Helens erupted?"

"I remember that." said Neil, "It was caused by the distortion in the atmosphere from the moisture and ash after the eruption."

I replied, "Rainbows are the result of a scientific happening. A rainbow is a reflection of the direct rays of the sun shining into our moisture laden atmosphere. These rays use the shiny, wet surface of the clouds behind as a mirror to reflect off of and appear as a rainbow in our skies."

"Yeah," Neil said, "it's a reflection of the sun's rays coming off of the force field that surrounds the earth. A rainbow is a direct reflection of that energy, but is reflecting only a portion of the force field. The rest of it is obscured always by the shadow of the earth. This is why rainbows are arched; the shadow of the earth is blocking the rest of the field."

"For a moment let's pretend that we can access the rest of the field of energy," I said. "Let's get on the magic rainbow carpet now and go with the TimeTraveler deep within the cosmos to the beginning of the TimeLine of Eternity. Here we will experience the events that led up to the 'big bang' which brought our universe into being."

The Perfect Vacuum

In the beginning there was nothing but a vacuum. This vacuum was in the ethereal realm to begin with. The original black hole or cocoon of ethereal matter of which you and I were a part, formed out of nothingness. A vacuum so intense with "nothing" will eventually produce a gaseous substance. This gaseous substance, the ethereal matter that forms because of the dark, freezing stillness, is another aspect of eternity, the same as the fact that there is no time or space in eternity. Where this matter came from or how it came about has no answer. It just was.

To explain further, although there was no atmosphere as we know it, there was a beginning of ethereal matter. This ethereal matter "sat" long enough that it began to deteriorate or rot. When something goes through this process it begins to give off a gas. This particular gas was odorless and colorless but was the beginning of an atmosphere. This atmosphere contained the ingredients to cause it to freeze. The freezing temperatures eventually began to "hatch," you might say, into different frequencies. These frequencies then begin to stir around and cause heat which allowed the process of forming a cocoon to take place. This cocoon consisted of all the frequencies reacting to each other and becoming stronger and stronger. This is when the tear in them took place.

The "ingredients," you might call them, of scientific elements were gases, causing frequencies combined with total darkness and freezing temperatures. This

3

combination in any lab today will cause a reaction of some kind depending on what gas is present. The gas that was present at the beginning is not available anywhere on the planet today, so these scientific reactions cannot be duplicated.

The darkness had a vibration to it. You see, absence of sound, or vibration, will eventually produce a vibration due to a natural tendency to want balance. With the "nothing" it wanted "something," so this "something" came into being as a vibration. A mixture of all potential colors of light (and corresponding musical tones) is what the darkness consisted of.

It is impossible for you and I to conceive of total darkness, stillness and freezing temperatures in physical matter being able to cause life, but this is exactly what it takes in the ethereal realm. The combination of these three items causes a coming to life of ethereal matter. These factors are as close as anyone is capable of giving to explain the beginning of creation. As far as where this first bit of ethereal matter originated, there is no explanation available.

Through those from the musical universe, I was given a look at the first evolving universe. By way of an explanation of each stage of build-up from the musical universe, I saw what took place as though from the inside of the events looking out. You were also part of this so I ask you to please put yourself in there with me as we go through the build-up leading eventually to the big bang.

The first phase of the budding universe was an endless, identical frequency of light that you and I were a part of. The absence of difference is what makes the basic building block for all things. As far as where this frequency of light came from, it just always was.

The second phase of the evolving universe was when the original vibration that we were part of, below the line of demarcation, caused a tear in the cocoon of ethereal matter that was the absolute beginning of all. In this case it tore away the skin containing the darkness, the black hole. This was the original black hole that has existed forever. Eternity is timeless. This black hole is still there in the exact same place. There is no time or space in eternity. It just is.

The third phase of the universe was when the cocoon unfolded its petals. It was an unfolding of "nothing;" it was complete stillness, frozen and dark that unfolded its petals like a tear in the lining of our universe which was caused by a vibration that came from the stillness.

The fourth phase of the universe came into being after the vibration caused the tear and the petals of this ethereal matter unfolded allowing the budding universe to rise above the line of demarcation – up from the internal dark hole into the manifested plane. This tiny little bit of vibration expanded to fill the total vacuum of allness that it found above the line of demarcation. This vacuum was not the same as you and I would picture a vacuum, because our vacuum denotes an absence of light. When this tiny bit of vibration rose up and expanded, the vacuum was filled with light – not visible light, but invisible and balanced light. Balanced light means an identical frequency throughout every square mile of eternity. It is difficult for us to picture an endless vacuum such as this because for me to even write about it defines it with borders in our mind. It had no borders then, it has no borders now. It just was. The best thing for us to compare it to is, perhaps, the air we breathe, the atmosphere of our particular domain. At this point the pressure forces caused the vacuum to form "condensation" inside its area of containment. The very frequency that filled the vacuum was so potent, so powerful, that it caused a heating up of the space above the line of demarcation. The space the vacuum filled was frozen before the light flooded it. This caused the condensation. When heat meets ice there is condensation. In this case it was droplets of condensed primal gas. This was the manifestation of the first physical matter in the entire universe. When the heat met the frozen nothingness it also caused a "whirlwind," so to speak, to develop. (We could compare this to the solar wind in our solar system.) This caused a buildup of air pressure and clouds that caused the forming of condensation inside the cloud, or bubble, of primal gases. There were two primal gases, hydrogen being one and what I will term "ash" because our planet has no name for it, being the other. It was totally absorbed during the coming explosion. It is found in rare bits of elemental matter but not on our planet.

The fifth stage was when the condensation inside the vacuum, which had actually started as one "droplet" or atom, split leaving two atoms or "droplets" of condensation bringing into being the manifestation of colors. This allowed these frequencies that filled the vacuum to express as beautiful, vibrating colors. The two atoms were infinitesimal in size, one positive and one negative, bringing about the first manifestation of male and female energies. Are you still with me and able to picture all this?

With the sixth stage, each universe was becoming more glorious than the previous one. The colors of the fifth universe, by their very vibrancy and beauty, brought about this sixth universe of atmospheric conditions that changed the colors into one glorious color of light, that of crystalline white. The atmospheric conditions were caused by the friction of the colors and the musical sounds combined.

The seventh stage was the actual beginning of creation. The potential of enormous growth and evolution was present in the fifth and sixth stages of the universe and produced atmospheric effects that manifested in matter as clouds. The clouds became surging, pregnant units of force made up of frequency. The vacuum became so great that it caused an implosion, a vacuum "sucking" into itself. After the seventh puff or cloud pulsation the build-up into glorious beauty could not be contained. It caused the stripping away of each universe in a receding order falling clear back to the beginning, only a transformed beginning. This transformed beginning started the identical buildup as before.

The first seven stages of the evolving universes were like seven puffs or pulsations of a mushroom cloud following an atomic bomb explosion. After the implosion of the seventh stage, the buildup leading to the explosion followed the same path as the first buildup.

This time the seven universes were patterned into the ether as basic shapes of evolution. The seven different phases all became separate universes even though none of them supported physical life as you and I know it until the seventh universe was reached. The other universes exist in time and space and have their own forms of life. Because they do exist as separate universes, I was given pictures of them and their position in respect to the line of demarcation, (shown in each drawing) including the musical tone and color they relate to. Everything that is given from the point of the "big bang" on takes place in the seventh universe – our universe, the one that we eventually ended up in.

Universe #1 – Potential Differentiation
Color of Red – Tone of C

Absence of Sound Will Produce a Vibration

Universe number one had only one mind, a large all-encompassing ability to know that it was the beginning and the end. This frequency was the frequency of universal thought before there were universes. There was nothing before this even frequency and there will be nothing after it. Nothing can ever disturb it, change it or stop it. This frequency encompasses and surpasses all frequencies. It permeates all things in all universes. This is called the Epicenter Frequency.

Even though this universe was of all one mind, the potential to separate the mind into fragments was preset in the beginning. This potential differentiation is a very important part of the evolutionary process. This first universe, then, was based on identical frequency throughout with the potential to change. The transformation of the first universe into the second universe depended on these two factors, frequency and potential or potential differentiation, being present in the beginning.

8

Universe #2 - Potential Force
Color of Orange – Tone of D

LINE OF DEMARCATION

Tear in Cocoon

Universe number two was born or created over a long period of endless time. Because there was no time as we know it, it was just "being," a state of stagnation combined with force. This is an upgrade situation from the first universe as it now becomes a matter of standing still while building the potential of expanding. Because the capabilities of this universe were locked into suspended animation, this second universe was blocked from realizing the possibility of becoming many different frequencies with many different rates of energy. This led to much frustration of the Creative Mind. This blockage caused the first hint of friction to come into being. The capabilities locked into suspended animation caused the combination of friction and force to combine into potential energy. We could term this universe as potential force. All things in all universes now have two building blocks combining matter (physical manifestation) and thought (spiritual manifestation).

Universe #3 - Potential Expansion
Color of Yellow – Tone of E

LINE OF DEMARCATION

The Cocoon Unfolded its Petals

The third universe is built on the building block called potential expansion for the possibility of outward movement of the original building blocks. It is made up of, under matter: differentiation, force and irritation; and under thought: potential, frustration and expansion. This is the third universe and this matter irritation combined with the thought of expansion brings about or accomplishes the next universe.

Universe #4 - Manifestation of Sound
Color of Green – Tone of F

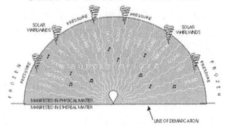

First Physical Matter

Universe number four was created from friction and expansion of the vacuum as described in universe number three. Know that the building blocks of the fourth universe are matter explosion or expansion, with thought relief, or end of frustration, or calmness, or balance. This new universe now has the immense capability of manifesting the combined aspects of matter which were formed in Universe #3 – differentiation, force and irritation (the positive or male aspects), into the aspects of thought, also formed in Universe #3 – potential, frustration and expansion (the negative or female aspects), and coming up with, or giving birth to, the Harmony of the Spheres. This fourth universe created the first sound as we know it. The universe before it had the potential to eventually do so but the actual manifestation of sound took place in the fourth universe. This manifestation of sound in physical matter took the form of a drop of condensation, the first matter in all of creation.

Universe #5 - Manifestation of Color
Color of Blue – Tone of G

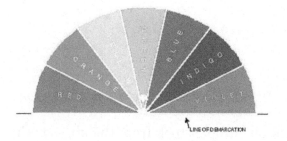

LINE OF DEMARCATION

First Polarity

The matter world, the drop of condensation, the first matter in the universe, was endlessly expanding and led to more frustration of thought because this sound needed a way to express its individuality. This was accomplished by the droplet of condensation splitting in half and bringing into being the manifestation of colors. This allowed these frequencies to express as beautiful, vibrating colors. Each different frequency took on a glow or emanation due to the combining of vacuum with vibration. Vacuum has a depth to it and vibration a motion. Vibration is movement. Frequency is this movement applied to sound – music, in other words and interpreted mathematically. This is the basis of the color kingdom, the beginning of a glorious universe.

Universe #6 - Crystalline White Light Fills Area
Color of Indigo – Tone of A

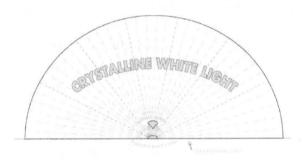

First Manifestation of Friction

What one droplet took from the air the other returned. One half pulled more vacuum into it through suction, (the negative or female droplet, which is the manifestation of color) and the other half gave back or emitted material of the vacuum back into the vacuum, (the positive or male droplet, the manifestation of sound). These two droplets or atoms continued pulling in and emitting until an imbalance was achieved. Due to the increasing vibration and the motion caused by the heat of the colors, a frequency was set up that continued to build until something had to give. It eventually overbalanced and crystalline white light filled the area – visible white light this time, not invisible as before. When the buildup of the seven universes reached the same point the second time the vacuum was unable to contain what had followed back into the tiny black hole.

Universe #7 - Nuclear Explosion
Color of Violet – Tone of B

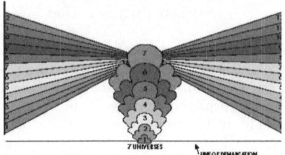

Explosion

The Big Bang

The droplets reunited and pushed the material contained in the droplets back out into what was left of the vacuum. This caused the explosion of the vacuum. The seven universes were like seven pulsations of a mushroom cloud following an atomic bomb explosion. We are

still in the action of the big explosion.

The explosion shattered all except one atom which was left perfect and whole, the hydrogen atom. This, then, was the birth of our Creator, the beginning of our universe, the seventh. You and I and everyone are "descended" you might say, from this seventh universe. We still have a long way to go in our travel on the timeline before we can actually reach anything we can relate to on a more personal level, but this is our "spiritual" family tree.

Nuclear Energy is God

The first nuclear explosion was actually what gave birth to our Creator. Nuclear energy is the Creator and, as such, is being misused. It should be worshiped and revered and respected because it is the Creator. The original split of the atom was done the first time the energy reached the seventh stage. The implosion then allowed the buildup to our universe, number seven, to take place. When you think of it this way perhaps you can see why our nuclear physicist's experiments are causing so much concern on the higher planets as far as the possibility of the splitting of the atom happening again.

Regardless, the original split of the atom came from so much time and space ago that it is forever collapsed into that tiny black hole at the center of creation.

Nuclear Explosion Compared to a Telescope

The explosion after the second buildup sent out twelve streamers from the very front of the explosion in which the chain reactions took place. To help you get a picture of

a chain reaction of a nuclear explosion, I'd like you to picture it as a telescope with sections that each fold into the other. The telescope originally extended out seven sections (the first seven stages of buildup) then collapsed back in. It then extended out to seven again (the second buildup) and twelve little telescopes went out from it this time – chain reactions in the nuclear explosion. We are in the action of one of these twelve streamers. These streamers are the galaxies. Twelve solar systems formed, or are forming, in each galaxy.

Seventh Universe Transforming Universe

The seventh universe of which our planet is a part is a transforming universe leading to the eighth universe, that of being one octave higher frequency than the first universe. It will have the same description as the first universe as being all the same, uniform frequency with one mind, only on an octave higher level. This new frequency will have embedded in it all that happened on the evolutionary journey from the first universe number one. This will give the frequency a depth and fulfillment and capacity for calmness; an enrichment that the first universe was incapable of having until it started on its path of transformation to an octave higher frequency.

Central Core is Life Force of All

It all starts with the tiny black spot at the center of

all universes. This tiny black spot is a tiny black hole of compressed space, and this is where the very high, most central, all powerful, original core of energy is to be

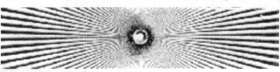

found. The central core of the universe is the life force of all in it. It is made up of frequencies of energies that are so high in pitch that one second of a sound of them would split earth in half. Such a high frequency of pitch or vibration is unknown on the earth. This central core is the energy center of those extremely high frequencies. This energy is the Harmony of the Spheres.

Chapter Two

THE DEVELOPMENT OF OUR UNIVERSE

Several years ago Neil and my husband and I had the opportunity to visit Alaska. One of the highlights of the trip was a helicopter ride over a glacier.

"Wow, this is awesome," Neil said with his voice full of excitement as our helicopter descended toward the glacier below us.

"I think glaciers are some of the most wondrous creations of nature," I responded.

The most memorable sights, the pictures that stayed with us, were the glimpses of beautiful blue ice that could be seen down inside the deep crevasses. The ice in glaciers is usually clear, coarsely crystalline and blue in color but there was a lot of dirt and debris on the top of this glacier due to volcanoes and other pollution.

"Look at that beautiful patch of blue ice and water down there to our left," Neil exclaimed."

"Some of these glaciers are very old," I said. "It's fascinating to me to think of a time when the whole planet was covered with ice during previous ice ages. Wouldn't it be interesting to experience the original ice age?"

We actually landed on the glacier itself for a few minutes. Our pilot didn't think we should stay very long because the weather looked threatening.

Neil & Helicopter on Glacier - Alaska

"Let's follow the TimeTraveler as he takes us on another incredible journey and allows us to experience the events that followed the 'big bang.' He'll take us back in time to the birth of the subatomic particles and the forming of the ice lattice, the superstructure of our universe," I said. "Let's ride the 'Carpet of Time' with him and using our imagination slide down inside one of the crevasses where we see the crystal blue ice," I continued. "We'll follow it back to the events that took place immediately after the big bang."

The Ice Lattice

Instead of dissipating, like a cloud in our sky will break up and disappear, the remnants of the fiery gas of

18

creation, hydrogen, were frozen for all time as they drifted off into the absolute zero degrees of the virgin outer space in which the big bang took place. Here they formed a superstructure over everything. This superstructure or crystalline lattice, then, is frozen hydrogen in outer space.

When something on earth is taken to absolute zero, this same crystalline lattice of frozen hydrogen will form over the substance you're working with as a protective shell to preserve the life of the atoms locked inside. (This is actually why our scientists have not been able to get anything down to absolute zero. This lattice forms at the crucial moment as it did at the beginning of creation in outer space, in the frozen reaches of time.)

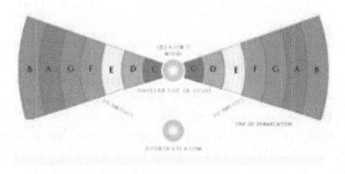

Lattice is Frozen Hydrogen

The Ice Lattice Superstructure

The attracting and repelling forces of the universe came into being and caused the very first subatomic particles that exploded out of the black hole to immediately rush or expand into the vacuum. As they did, the process of forming a skim of ice took place as they cooled in the outer reaches of space. Thus began the clumping together that formed an ice superstructure or lattice for the universes. As each of the seven explosions took place this superstructure was pushed further and further out to the sides of empty space and grew thicker and stronger with each explosion and more densely frozen each time it was pushed further and further into the outer reaches. This formed boundaries out to the side of our universe. No matter exploded above or below the black hole. The bottom of the black hole, the bottom of our universe in other words, is for all-time leading into the black hole of condensed matter.

Lattice Formation Similar to Ice in Tray

To explain this ice lattice think of a slice of crystal or a thin piece of ice formed over water. One is, after all, the same as the other with the exception that the crystal has been hardened or solidified by intense, fast heat. It was instantaneous fusion of the atoms that made up the crystals on our planet. They are indeed drops of frozen moisture hardened or fused by heat. They were not frozen water; they were drops of condensation of gases.

An example of a lattice would be the forming of ice crystals in a tray of water. It is the coming together in a "like attracts like" manner of freezing subatomic particles. When the temperature gets almost to the freezing point the particles rise in an effort to find heat, the heat that gave them birth. Failing to find heat they cling together and attract more to rise from the freezing liquid and join them, always in an attempt to find heat.

Universes Vibrated to C Major Scale

A lattice will form into patterns determined by the particles themselves. Each gas formed into its own frozen lattice with its own pattern and formed seven structures of contained universes. Out beyond these seven universes is the superstructure of the whole universe. Within each of the seven structures of lattices the suns began their reflecting off of the angles created by the lattice and formed musical tones. The superstructure over the whole universe vibrates to the tone of C. Because it is still embedded in the black hole, the first universe also had the same tone, that of C. The second universe had a higher tone, that of D, as the result of its sun being reflected off the crystal lattice. It was influenced by the superstructure itself and tied to it as the second tone of a scale that had vibratory relationship and structure and meaning to it that involves music theory. The next universe formed the tone E, and so on up to the seventh universe, our universe, which formed the tone of B. All of these universe tones were caused by suns in the outside, between the universes and the superstructure of the total universe.

These suns threw the reflections of the whole superstructure downward into the seven universes and colored the smaller suns within the seven universes with the different vibrations of the facets of the superstructure. Our universes will not be complete until the new universe, the eighth, is formed – the octave higher C. We are on the brink of it now.

Each universe formed a lattice of twelve "corners," if you will, because of the refraction from the superstructure, and each solar system formed in its own corner of the lattice. There is a distinct order to these solar systems. The lattice is responsible for the vibrations. Without the ice structure to reflect off of, the initial light would have scattered out into the far reaches of the universe. The forming of the superstructure allowed containment of the light and reflection of the light, without which there could have been no vibrations and therefore no life forms.

Lattice of Ice Formed at Big Bang

To recap, the whole universe formed into a crystalline lattice at the time of the big bang. It is in the forming of the lattice that we find the necessary processes to give birth to new creations. The grid map that we have over our planet is a small part of this crystalline lattice of the universe. The rays of the suns between the universes and the superstructure strike the crystalline lattice containing each universe and cause several reactions to take place. To begin with, it separates the universe into a network of vibratory fields which manifest in different dimensions. These dimensions then operate and grow and evolve within their own vibratory field.

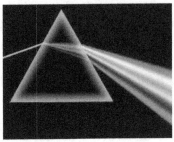
Picture it as a crystal or diamond that the sun shines on. Each facet of the crystal will give off or emit the colored light of its particular musical tone. There are twelve musical tones in each crystalline lattice that formed at beginning creation. These lattices are made up of ice that formed out of the superstructure of the explosion. They

became frozen streams of time and space. This was the theory behind the huge crystal at Atlantis.

Ice Lattice Similar to Crystal at Atlantis

The Crystal of Atlantis was dark red but had a mottled look, showing dark and light spots in the inside. It was fairly large in size, about thirty feet in diameter at the bottom, narrowing in to perhaps five feet at the crown. It was based on mathematics; it was faceted according to the mathematical calculations of the course of the sun. It did not track by turning but tracked the sun by faceting. Because the sun was constantly moving, this involved a series of facets so fine as to be almost one solid ring around the crystal. And there was more than one ring. There were seven rings around the crystal all faceted or carved with the most intricate, precision-like cuts. The cuts caught the sun's rays and each ring caught them differently according to its pattern.

The reflected auras of the crystal were then caught and harnessed at different areas of the land. The channels between each facet allowed maximum storage of the ray in any particular area at one time. Then it would be picked up by the next "station." One ring was for air transportation, one was for communication with space ships, one was for energy to run pumping systems for irrigation purposes, one was for growing food itself and the final one, as far as being useful to everyone, was for healing the people. There was one more that was used for secret work by the priests. The topmost ring itself was used to energize the crystal so the other six rings were more potent than they would have been without the seventh or top ring. It was an accentuator ring.

The color of red came from the stone the crystal was carved from. It was polished and the surface was smooth with all the intricate faceting being on the underneath side. If the facets had been directly exposed to the sun it would immediately have caused havoc in all the land due to the chaotic and powerful rays that would have been shooting off the crystal. The only way to control it was to have the facets on the underneath side and then control them with the accentuating ring at the top of the crystal. This was all mathematically designed. The stone that was used was brought from another planet. There is no such stone available on the earth today.

Lattice Preserved Atomic bits of Matter

Because this lattice formed over the substance of which our universe was made, it preserved the integrity of the atomic bits of matter, you and me. In other words, we were not destroyed; we were allowed to live and to start the process of evolution because of the protective crystalline lattice.

At the implosion when the two droplets fused, splatters of droplets were moved off from them, some before the fusion, which accounts for either negative or positive particles, and some even after they fused, which accounts for neutral or fused particles. They were drawn into the black hole of implosion in this form of already being either male, female or fused. They were then blasted back out in intense heat. This caused instant hardening into individual particles programmed for all time, locked inside of their beingness as either positive, negative or fused energies.

24

These are our subatomic particles, the protons, neutrons and electrons. The first implosion drew these particles into the frozen reaches below the line of demarcation. At this time they were exposed to an intense blast of heat, a very quick burst of heat that crystallized them.

This is when the subatomic particles went into a state of stoppage of activity, a transitory time for them, but programmed into them were the electrical impulses of vibrations that they were part of when the first two droplets of moisture came together.

Motion Patterns of the Subatomic Particles

The subatomic particles were our forebears remember, and they evolved through many different stages of evolution. The original universe that led to the 1st superuniverse number seven started as a vacuum inside of which condensation formed. This universe was in the shape of a triangle. The particles started their evolutionary growth inside this triangular shaped vacuum, moving in a triangular pattern.

After the second buildup and the following explosion, the triangular shaped universe moved out of its three pointed shape into a round shape and the particles started moving in this manner. The third universe is shaped in a rectangular pointed shape. It represents the basic structure of building blocks on the earth's surface.

As far as why these patterns are important, they lay out the pattern or shape of the crystalline structure of our elements, determining how they will combine to make minerals and how the energy will travel in the Prismatic Kingdom. An element will be the basic shape of the universe that it originated in. Some elements originated in the first universe and have the triangle bases, some in the second universe with the circle, etc. These basic shapes stay with the element when it combines with bits of ash or matter to form other elements. These shapes are very important to total understanding of the new technology that makes up the projects in the Science of Music (which will be discussed in a future volume of the notebooks).

These patterns need to be on the earth plane for future reference. The patterns we are now using will need to be replaced due to damaging future technology. This is what is going to begin happening more and more. One part of technology cannot be refined and carried into the fourth dimension without all other aspects that work with it (and need to be in harmony with it) being brought into line with fourth dimensional technology. A study needs done on our present electricity, as to the vibrational patterns now in place. Drawings could be made of the amps in our present electricity which would show an evolution or development but not to the extent that the new electricity will develop. The patterns in place now are not so intricate.

This does not have to do with voltage or wattage, but rather with amperes of electricity, which is a more basic form of electricity than we receive in our homes. This will be found at the power plants as the stage electricity is in before being channeled into the form we use in our homes.

Particles Experienced Many Different Patterns

Vibratory rates create pictures, as well as sound, in all dimensions. This composes a language of vibration that could be studied and used as a universal language. The patterns are slightly different for each dimension due to evolving of the particles. They progressed through the universes with a different pattern of movement and expression in each one. These thinking pin points of subatomic particles moved through all kinds of experiences in all the other universes before coming to our universe, the seventh.

Some of the things they experienced are simply not fathomable by you and I. In some universes, they traveled constantly on their educational path. They do this traveling individually and in a set, predetermined pattern. Sometimes they are in a motion of spiking; sometimes they twirl, other times they are on a silent, smooth glide. They learn to conform to the traffic patterns they come into contact with and to never cause a collision. But there are many other things they learn. For example, one thing that they work diligently on in the third universe is increasing and decreasing their intensity at will.

Each universe has its lessons and its goals, just as each of the planets have their lessons and goals. Each individual subatomic particle has a distinctive pattern of motion that, when grouped with other particles, causes a "group" motion. Remember that all of this is part of our divine heritage.

Atoms Made Up of Particles

The atom is a frozen drop of condensation, made up of the tiny little droplets of vibratory rates, the subatomic particles, which are mixtures of all the vibratory rates. The allocation of each mixture is what determines what kind of an atom it is. Each of these tiny bits of vibrational pieces of the original explosion is still vibrating. Remember, they were saved from extinction because of the crystal lattice that formed. As given previously, some of them are positive vibratory droplets, some negative and some are fused droplets of both positive and negative that happened at original creation. The fission of the explosion resulted in some cases of fusion.

Even as the one Creator of all was fused into positive and negative for all time, so also were varying degrees of size of the result of this explosion. Not everything fused, but many did and in all different size scale levels. The subatomic particles are the smallest size scale products of fusion and the large suns in our universe are the largest examples of fusion. This is why they are capable of giving life, because they are fused male and female energies therefore are prolific. Anything that is pure male or pure female vibrations will always be barren. Therefore, the process of life itself is fusion.

Sun is Large Atom

The atom is a drop of condensation that has hardened into a tiny bead. It is a frozen bead of moisture from original creation. At each step of its life it has been fed from the eternal spring of vibrations that are coming into the lattice through our sun. Our sun is a large atom, a replica of the original hydrogen atom that has sunk into a black hole.

There were many splits off of the original atom and each one of them formed its own hierarchy. The splitting of the atom in the completed form of the process, explained previously in the nuclear explosion did not take

28

place with any but the original or there would be no universes manifesting. They would all be sunk into black holes which are inversions of manifested time and space. There is a line of demarcation, as spoken of before, where everything under this line is enclosed eternally into its internal self. Above this line of demarcation everything is manifested outwardly.

Suns are Generators of Particles

The one atom that was left pure and whole and fused is smaller, but more powerful than anything that expanded off of it, even though what expanded off from it is enormous in size by comparison. Those that were fused were the more powerful and expanded greatly because fusion will always be strength. These became the suns that were able to generate the strength or heat of fusion and continue to give birth to particles that began to fill up all space. All the many suns are generators of particles. They are all givers of life to the universe.

Polarity

To review thus far, a subatomic particle is a bit of frozen, or hardened vibratory rate programmed at beginning creation with either a positive or negative vibration due to the fission of the explosion, or it is a neutral vibratory rate, fused male and female vibrations, due to fusion that took place at original creation. This, of course, is what we call the neutron. The proton is the positive (male) energy and the electron is the negative (female) energy. The female energy is programmed for all time to be the instigator of life and evolvement of all things. The male energy is programmed for all time to be the steady central core that is connected to the sun as the father of all life.

Planets are Male Energy - Stars Female

The female energies banded together as did the male energies. The male energies were more stable and became the planets, the female energies being weaker formed stars and the nebulae that will eventually form into stars. The stability of planets is the male energy that attracts stars and nebulae (female energies) to themselves. The female energies are constantly shifting and forming into star material. This continues to take place until enough female energy has come together to have the power and force to be a star. They are not suns; they are not instigators of life at this point. They must be attracted to a planet strongly enough to give off a flare or comet to send to that planet and this will instigate other forms of life on the planet. Most people think of the planets as female. In truth the planets are strong, stable, male or positive energy. The female energy of the stars is causing the formation of the new universe, the eighth. It is also mostly the female energy on our planet that is instigating the new teachings to help the planet evolve into the next octave of evolution.

Fission and Fusion

To add a bit more about fission and fusion, fusion will be the result of harmony and will result in harmony. This is "like attracts like" in one of its manifestations at the primal level. Fission will always be the result of

30

disharmony and will result in disharmony. The original bits of vibratory rate that did not fuse were at disharmony with all they bumped into in the virgin universe because of the force of the energy behind them. It mattered not whether they were positive or negative, they simply couldn't blend with each other due to the fierceness and ferociousness of the original explosion. Those that did fuse did so before they reached the outer virgin territory. They fused while still within the process of the explosion. They can never be separated. The attracting and repelling forces of the universe eventually allowed the positive energy, the male to become dominant. Positivity will always be dominant over negativity on our planet. Therefore, the proton, male energy, attracted into its orbit the female or negative energy.

Expanded Musical Scales Give More Vibratory Rates

The lattice allows each dimension that formed from the different facets to be fed or nourished from all the vibratory rates, even though their particular facet is only one of the twelve vibratory rates. We now have twelve vibratory rates but, as given previously, there are more vibratory rates to be "heard" from in the future. This will be in the form of the expanded scales.

The Science of Music is used throughout the universe, but the higher planets are working on expanded scales. Earth is not and will not be able to be in tune with the universe until she is also working on the expanded scale. She cannot move forward to accomplish the expanded scale until all are in tune with earth's seven tone major scale and the twelve tone chromatic scale. This must be the starting point.

Seven Tone Scale

In the beginning creation was whole, based on the seven tone major scale.

C-D-E-F-G-A-B

Twelve Tone Chromatic Scale

Then, when restructured creation came into being, the twelve tone chromatic scale was begun and it was divided in half, (male and female), then into thirds, (the trinity - our mind, our past lives and the universal mind), now it is to be divided into fourths, (synthesized man - physical, emotional, mental and spiritual bodies), for the fourth dimension.

C-C#/Db-D-D#/Eb-E-F-F#/Gb-G-G#/Ab-A-A#/Bb-B

Expanded Musical Scales

Fifteen Tone Scale

Future restructuring of the human being can be seen by going into an expanded scale which will add three tones making a fifteen tone scale which will be divided into five sections for basing lessons on.

C-C1/2-C#/Db-D-D#/Eb-E-F-F1/2-F#/Gb-G-G1/2-G#/Ab-A-A#/Bb-B

Eighteen Tone Scale

Then by adding three more making an eighteen tone scale, the lessons will be divided into six.

C-C1/2-C#/Db-D-D1/2-D#/Eb-E-E#/Fb-F-F1/2-F#/Gb-G-G1/2-G#/Ab-A-A#/Bb-B-B#/Cb

Twenty-One Tone Scale

By adding three more to make a twenty-one tone scale the lessons will be divided into seven.

C-C1/2-C#/Db-D-D1/2-D#/Eb-E-E1/2-E#/Fb-F-F1/2-
F#/Gb-G-G1/2-G#/Ab-A-A1/2-A#/Bb- B-B1/2-B#Cb

These expanded scales are what will be reached when the gases are taken to absolute zero on our planet. The new lattices that will form will be the new half steps that will expand the scale from twelve to fifteen, eighteen and then twenty-one tones. The first ones to be expanded and used of these new lattices will be hydrogen, nitrogen and oxygen. Then the expansion of helium, neon and xenon will take place.

There will still be more to be added. The first three will expand the scale to fifteen, the next three to eighteen and the last three, which haven't been manifested yet on the earth will form into the twenty-one tone scale. The new gas that will result from technology based on the Science of Music (The SolarSelect Project discussed in Vol. 9 of the notebooks) will be the first of this last trio.

Inert Gases Basis for Active Gases

To recap, the crystalline lattice that formed over the gases at beginning creation preserved the molecular action of the inert gases and separated them into enclosed units that all had a mixture of the primal gases in them. These mixtures then began a process of decomposition, you might say, which led to new formation of gases. The decomposition of the inert gases led to the forming of the active gases.

Even from the beginning of the universe the process of evolution remains ever the same – the new is built upon the old in an upgraded form. Therefore, the inert gases are, as a matter of fact, the basis of the new active gases that formed. The cause of this birth was the protective shell of the crystalline lattice. This lattice kept the gases of each particular facet from spreading. In other words, it set a limit of their expansion thereby allowing or causing interaction between the gases and the light being reflected off of the lattice by the original explosion. This light eventually sank or collapsed into the black hole where the tiny, tiny original atom that came about because of the explosion is still churning forth its energy that is bubbling up out of this black hole for all time. It is the generator of the life forces for all reaches of all universes. Ours is the seventh universe.

Grid over Earth is Shadow of Original Ice Lattice

Within our particular structure the process of "like attracts like" began and certain mixtures of vibrations were attracted to other mixtures of vibrations forming into clumps which eventually separated into the suns and planets. Our solar system formed and also all others, in their own corner of the lattice structure. As each solar system formed and the cooling process continued, lighter weight versions of the lattice formed to cover them.

The lighter weight lattices consisted of shadows or remnants or ghosts of the original lattice and these shadows attracted a formation of ethereal matter. In other words, the grid over our planet is a shadow of a larger grid over our whole solar system. This is a shadow

34

of the original superstructure of our universe – the ice crystal lattice that formed at original creation.

Light Reflections cause Male, Female and Blended Energy

The coming together of vibratory patterns that cause male, female or blended energy is simply a reflection of light off of the lattice. It is a mathematical happening. The slant of the particular surface of the lattice that the sun is striking determines the vibration that is sounded from the meeting of the light ray and the reflecting surface, which eventually produces a tiny drop of condensation.

If the reflection is from a left-slanted piece of the lattice it is male energy, a positive charge on the atom. If reflecting off a right-slanted piece of lattice it is female energy, a negative charge. If the light is hitting a forty-five degree angle it is a blended energy charge, our neutrons.

When the light reflects off the lattice at certain points the whole array of vibratory rates of the scale is available and programs the bit of condensation with all the vibrations. These are the males. They are not as numerous as the females because the females are formed of single bits of vibration. This is why the male is positive energy - because it is a completed scale. The female is negative energy because it is only one single vibratory rate of the scale.

It is simply a matter of light reflection that causes positivity or negativity. In the human brain the same thing is true. A female will be inclined to draw in negativity due to using the right side of the brain and a male will tend the opposite, to draw in positivity due to using the left side of the brain. When these entities learn to use the cross brain method of approaching thinking they will tend to draw in blended energy because of the light reflecting the crisscross pattern that occurs when both sides of the brain are incorporated.

This is the point that humans must strive to reach. Anything that will cause a usage of the combined sides of the brain is excellent. Music fills this bill very nicely as it must be based on structured disciplines and then refined with expression or unstructured disciplines coming from the right brain. For a final performance, there must be a blending between the left brain structure and the right brain non-structure.

Core of Atom is Male, the Shells are Female

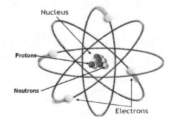

"Nuclear Structure" of the Atom

Nucleus

Protons

Neutrons

Electrons

The shells of the atoms are orbits of the female energy around the balanced core. This core consists of the male and the neutral energies. Because the neutral energy, the neutron, is half male, this, combined with the total male energy of the proton, serves as an overbalance of male energy. This, in itself, requires more female energy to need to be attracted. Because the female energy is in motion it is not as strong as the central core which is stationary. This causes the need for even more female energy.

The best way to describe it is to split the male energy into eight pieces and the neutral energy into eight pieces. Half of the neutron is female and half is male so this would give us a total of twelve bits of male energy.

The females will need to be eight in number and when combined with the four bits of female energy from the neutron, make up twelve bits of female energy. The female energy is on a ratio of eight electrons to complete a scale while the male has the complete scale within himself with the neutron giving the extra four to bring it to a twelve tone scale when the time comes for this to happen. For the time being all is based on the eight tone completed scale. This is the way the proton is programmed.

Patterns for Human Behavior come from Atoms

The female is a better transmitter due to being a single point of energy, whereas the male would not be quite as clear due to over-frequencies. These over-frequencies are also why he is attracted to all females while the female being a single frequency is attracted to only one frequency within the makeup of a given male, the dominant frequency in that male, that is exposed externally.

The male, on the other hand is equally balanced internally with all vibrations, so all females are attractive to him.

However, it quite often happens more often than not, as a matter of fact, that

the dominant externally expressed frequency is quite often attracted to the female wearing this frequency and therefore two that are compatible do match up.

It depends on the strength of the internal remainder of vibratory rates as to how the male chooses to react to other females. The stronger the internal life of a male, the more attraction other females will have for him. If the internal life is not progressed the male will most likely be content in a monogamous relationship. Therefore, the more evolved and open spiritually with the inner life, the more frequent the attractions to other females are. A lesser evolved male will be content with his matching vibratory rate female.

A female who is growing and evolving and expanding will not be content with a less evolved male and will be attracted to the more evolved male and will need to understand that his internal makeup and growth and evolvement will always cause him to seek all female vibrations until he settles into his true mission in life and begins externally expressing the dominant vibration for his mission.

This may happen several times that he will want to change females, say every time he moves into a new area of fulfilling his spiritual mission. Therefore, if a man changes profession he will eventually most likely change females. When he steps to a higher mission-related career he will most likely change females again.

The man who stays in one job most of his life, or at least does not constantly grow into new and more challenging positions serving him as spiritual growth material, will be content with one woman. On the other hand, the woman who is a single vibratory rate and will remain so all her life must constantly strive to fill the remainder of the scale she is expressing with elusive tendencies of all the other vibrations.

This is the drive of the female electrons to fill the shell. A female will steadily increase the intensity of her single-minded vibration as she grows and evolves, and eventually will grow past the male who is not growing and will be attracted to a male who is externally expressing her vibration as his dominant manifested vibration for that stage of his spiritual mission of evolvement.

Human Relationships Patterned after Particles

The subatomic particles are free floating in the air as part of our atmosphere. We are surrounded by them; we move and breathe in a "soup" of them. There is an unending supply of them.

When the time comes to start a new shell there will be so many clamoring to be the one chosen that it will be chaos until the strongest wins out. This battle over being the one who wins the male is patterned into the female energy and is reflected in female humans.

The relationship between human behavior and the makeup of atoms will readily show where the patterns for male and female behavior had their beginnings. Humans are, after all, a manifestation of the Creator's energy, the same as all evolution is. All life, action and behavior are a repeated pattern.

Chapter Three

THE BIRTH OF OUR GALAXY

Neil and I were driving across the barren desert of eastern California, returning from a vacation in Colorado. "Aren't clouds fascinating?" I asked Neil "Have you ever just sat and watched them drift across the sky? Sometimes they drift together and form one large cloud. Other times they separate and each goes its own way. At times you can make out different shapes such as animals in them."

Clouds

41

"I can remember doing that when I was young and we were traveling in the car," Neil said. "Since I started working with photography I'm more apt to notice their colors now than their shapes. Many times they are absolutely a brilliant white or tinged with silver. Other times they are pink or lavender. Still at other times they can be dark and foreboding."

I replied, "Once a friend sent me a photo of a cloud that looked just like a butterfly." As I got my water bottle from the cooler, I said, "The material that drifted off after the big bang was made up of subatomic particles. It acted in exactly the same manner as clouds, but it was actually a thinking mass of subatomic particles – the first Mind."

Getting excited, Neil responded, "Can you imagine being the first one on a world where no one had ever been before? This Mind would not have known anything other than feeling good and being happy and joyous."

"Yes," I said, "This Mind, feeling all of this intellectually, would then have influenced everything that came after this with these feelings of freedom, curiosity, joy, peace, happiness, etc. These feelings would be embedded in all the planets, stars, and even the nebulae that are still forming, especially the nebulae because they have never seen anything other than this pure Mind."

Neil replied, "Yeah, they would have formed into pure, clear, uncluttered, unpoisoned bodies until the process of evolution starts. The very process of evolution itself would be the cause of the vibration being lowered. This is a scientific happening."

I said, "That's because the lowering of the vibration causes a cluttering of the mind which in turn causes the lowering of the vibration. All of us from evolutionary worlds will always face this battle. There is no way to overcome it as long as evolution continues, except through education as to the cause of it all. Through the magic of the TimeTraveler, using our imagination, let's climb aboard one of the larger clouds in the sky and drift off into the cosmos back to the events that took place after the big bang had released these subatomic particles into the universe. Let's let the TimeTraveler take us on an incredible journey that will help us understand the Mind of the Creator."

The First Mind

When the original explosion occurred, at that time there was a "Mind," the Creator's Mind. The excitement of the explosion, the sheer awe and wonder of this Mind, this first "thinking" being, with a body of energy for a form, was what caused the creation of everything and the tiny little central core that caused it all is still there. This is very difficult for us on the earth plane to grasp.

Hydrogen Atom Compared to a Pearl

An analogy here might be to compare the tiny atom that is still at the center of all creation to the grain of sand that's still in the center of the pearl as the pearl formed around it.

The first Mind was developed, remember, in the original cocoon of vacuum by the beginning vibrations and was given birth into beingness during the explosion. This Mind expanded and set the pattern for all to come afterwards; all that has taken place since then originated in this Mind. These particles were once the "complete Mind" of the Creator that was present in the black hole beneath the Line of Demarcation. At the time of the nuclear explosion this Mind was shattered into individual particles.

You and I and everyone were part of one of these particles. Due to the principle of "like attracts like" the particles grouped together as far as vibration went and began to form into galaxies, stars, planets and suns.

Much of the original mind stayed contained within the black hole beneath the Line of Demarcation and controlled or patterned the particles that were drifting away into the vast cosmos with a pattern for the perfect mind.

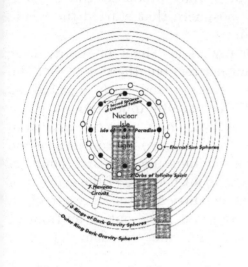

The area in the vacuum where the explosion took place is the Nuclear Isle of Light. When the vacuum was shattered into endlessness, part of the central nucleus of energy, the main Creator, or God if you will, was torn away and settled into a pattern of revolution around this stationary core. Universal drift then took control and creation worked its way ever outward from the tiny droplet. It is all forever expanding outward away from the original Creator God.

Thoughts can Travel Anywhere

The same as your thoughts can travel anywhere, the thoughts of this first Mind are constantly revolving, not only around the core but are being solidified into the forming of matter bodies – the planets and stars. Lesser clouds of energy were caught in the current and drifted and still are drifting into endlessness. Some of them clump and cling together and form solid bodies of light and matter. Some just drift. These were lesser "Gods" or "Creators" who paid homage to the "Inner God or Creator" that they knew was their origin. Some have captured more of the light energy than others, but all were once the same body of nothingness that produced the original droplet of condensed atmosphere that started the whole pattern of everlasting life.

There are, indeed, many lesser "Gods" or "Lords" over these bodies of light and matter, but there is, truly, one central, divine nuclear energy God with a mind so powerful that none can ever hope to understand it, much less have direct contact with it. There is no comparison to anything on any planet that can give you an idea of the power and glory of this minuscule starting point of everything. Its size comes about because of the concept of compressed time and the expansion of the universe of all who leave this central core and move out away from it, growing and expanding in the freedom of vast endlessness.

The esoteric meaning of a black hole is simply the inner, esoteric part of anything, the part that you can't see, the thought-form. When we go to the inner planes at the end of a lifetime, esoterically speaking we have gone into a black hole, a mini-black hole. Planets do the same thing; the Creator did the same thing. He is in His inner planes; has never left His inner planes, is perhaps a better way of saying it.

Never having left the inner planes and gone out into the universe that was expanding away from Him because of the explosion, He has no way of learning, or growing or expressing except through what went off of Him at the time of the explosion. There are little

fine filaments connected to everything (even us) that exploded off of that mini-black hole, the Creator God, the central core of powerful churning energy. These tiny filaments of thread, the Creator's thoughts, go to every part of the Creator God's universe; umbilical cords, if you will, still connected to the planets.

Creator's Development and Birth Compared to Humans

The Mind of the Creator is made up of scientific reactions to exoteric events – instinctual behavior reactions that can't be changed due to the laws of scientific reactions.

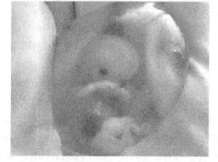

The Creator's development was of scientific reactions. His birth is another story. The same is true of humans. Our development in the womb is a scientific chain of events that can only be altered by the most drastic of events, among which is chemical poisoning.

When the Creator was developing there was no such thing as chemicals to poison any part of His development. Therefore, He is the most pure development of

anything that could ever be possible.

When He was born the Mind came into being as a thinking entity. This Mind was unpoisoned and uncluttered because there was nothing to poison or clutter it. Everything was absolutely pure and clean. Therefore, this Mind followed absolute perfection as far as reaction to scientific circumstances. It is still so.

The human mind, on the other hand, is subject to poison and clutter from the first moments of birth on. This is due to evolution. Creation will always be pure – evolution will always be impure. Even though evolution is a scientific reaction to circumstances also, it is subject to influence. Pure creation is not subject to influence by others. Remember this at all times.

This Mind of the Creator is capable of feelings, but only of clear, clean, uncluttered, unpoisoned feelings. These are the feelings that high vibrations will bring. The higher and finer the vibration of our bodies, the cleaner and clearer are our feelings. It is as simple as that. When the vibration is low the disharmony results in grating, grinding vibrations that cause pain in the mind. The first Mind had no way of experiencing these low vibrations. They simply weren't there. The original vibration was high and fine and this caused the first Mind to feel joy at being, curiosity about who He was and where He was and what exactly He was supposed to do now.

The Master Universe with all its different worlds is an exact pattern of the growth and development of the human mind, starting with physical evolution, and proceeding through the changes brought in the human mind by the insemination of genes from higher kingdoms The inner circles are the ultimate goal over many lifetimes, but the outer circles show the exact pattern of

48

study and learning that needs to be gone through for each human to progress in each lifetime.

Cells of Humans Patterned after the Master Universe

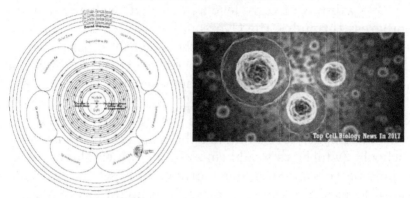

The repeated pattern of the universe is evident in the growth, physically and spiritually of the human universe, as each entity is patterned after one in a higher world that is a pattern of the highest. As spoken of before, the pattern of one cell in the human physical body is an exact pattern of the Master Universe. One cell in the spiritual thinking process will follow the thinking, reasoning and worshipping process of the entities in that Master Universe.

Twelve Stepping-Stones of our Solar System

Earth still receives most help and teaching from more advanced planets. She is a baby, a mere suckling infant in the overall scheme of even the immediate solar system. The twelve stepping stones of our immediate solar system are suspended animation, impregnation, incubation, and after this one (earth) of education will be hibernation, and appreciation, to be followed by illumination and eventually by the stages of fraternization and experimentation, then by perceptulization, adoration and Christulization or crystallization

We will have twelve levels in each of twelve planets to progress through – the Oversoul has twelve trips through twelve solar systems – all in the seventh superuniverse. Therefore, a total complete study of the pattern of evolvement and growth throughout eternity is the pattern each individual life must follow.

When we graduate from the Central Core we reside in the outer-space levels and are the teachers in the primary schools, (which we would consider our inner planes when applying this to our inner journey), only we are working on a level of pre-thought forms. You might say the outer space levels are the incubator stages for Oversouls.

The primary schools exist for the sake of instigating thought-forms in the matter universe. There are, at present, only four outer space levels, but there will be more, as needed, up to seven. This is in the Master Universe. Here we gather together the blend of virtues and graces and make a pool of energy that the Oversoul can use as His "body" when He begins His journey. This is very complicated and only serves to confuse unless it can be simplified.

Oversoul Compared to Granary

Let's take an example of a granary where all the different grains with their individual qualities are gathered. One farmer (Oversoul) comes to the granary and takes so many sacks of each different grain (atoms) to

His own farm (Universe) to have it stored there to be used as He needs and sees fit.

•The outer space levels are the original fields of grain. The superuniverse is the granary and God is the Master Controller of the granary. The Oversoul is the farmer and we are one of the pieces of grain. This is as simple as needs be to explain this part.

•The superuniverse, the intermediate school, is where the grain is stored until it is needed. These are the evolutionary worlds. The outer space worlds are not evolutionary, they are manifest eternally.

•The superuniverses – the evolutionary worlds or the intermediate schools – are where the qualities of the different grains are tested and crossed and mixed and worked on until as perfect as they can become in this intermediate school.

•They then continue to work their way to the Central Core and then back out into outer space as a teacher in the original field of grain, trying at all times to produce better crops of basic grain, better stock (atomic matter) to be sent to the superuniverse for intermediate schooling.

Other Superuniverses

There is no crossing permanently into the life activities of the other superuniverses, even though we are brought abreast of their knowledge and ways of thinking and progressing and can, and do, communicate with them. We can never become one of them when we originate on an evolutionary world.

As mentioned before, we will never fully understand those from the other superuniverses, but will love them regardless for their differences and similarities. Those from strictly spiritual origin can and will be able to blend with and become part of any of the seven superuniverses.

Four Outer Space Levels
Relate to Stages of Awareness

The four outer space circles can also be related directly to the stages of growth a person must go through as the primary stages of awareness.

1. Of these four stages the first is the awakening to the knowledge that there is more than organized religion has to offer.

2. The second stage usually leads directly to occult practices.

3. The third stage moves on to psychological search.

4. And the fourth stage, that of finding the true path as being that of the universal brotherhood, leads one on to the intermediate schools (the superuniverses discussed in the previous paragraph) which then helps one learn to better understand their brothers.

Can you see the importance of tracing this progression? As the spiritual center (Central Core) of our being is attained, we then return to the outer space circle to teach and aid those on the upward spiral. Now none of this is acquired in a single lifetime, of course, for anyone, but as everything is a repeated pattern for all else, each lifetime should pattern itself after this process as far as spiritual growth is concerned. In other words like a mini-course in the University of Life, (our universe.)

After the first trip through the Central Core, most likely we will start again in not only the same universe, but also the same galaxy.

After progressing through the solar system we are in now and twelve others, we will proceed inward to the Central Core.

When we start again we will start in another solar system in our local galaxy and proceed through twelve solar systems and back into the center.

This will continue forever. We will eventually return to our original solar system and start all over again. As given previously, we do not cross over into other superuniverses, ever.

Our Education Should Follow Progress of Central Universe

The process of education followed throughout the Central Universe, shows the variety of education and growth that is needed on the earth plane. A quick scan of that process should be enough to convince anyone that one life on the earth plane simply will not do it.

As each progressive sphere on the inner circuit is traversed, it is directly related to each incarnation on the earth plane. The study of the seven circles is important because this is a micro plan that should be brought into macro focus and applied to stages of the path for each individual. The whole layout of education and progress of the universe is exactly the same as each individual layout. But it is real and on an ever-increasing applicable status as progress is made. However, schooling should always be based on this inward journey and each life on earth needs to see some progress comparable to universal stages of progress.

When the Oversoul leaves this solar system for the next He will be a much wiser Oversoul, but will follow the same pattern of shattering and synthesizing that is followed in our solar system.

To recap, as He moves through the inner circuit, He skips none of the circles, but one will be easier for Him as it will contain the spirit of the superuniverse He traversed through. He will not enter any of the other six superuniverses, but will gain the knowledge they gained from their point of view of the overseeing spirit of that superuniverse by each of the inner circuits.

When reaching the Central Core, He is sent to the section reserved for those from His particular superuniverse to reside, but is not kept from associating with others.

Each one forms their own group who then, in turn, help the reincarnation and recirculation of life on planets in their own superuniverse.

Oversoul Then Moves On

The Oversoul Himself, then moves on. The Oversoul Himself is progressing through all stages of the path in this manner, that of splitting and rejoining. Even when reaching the Central Core, He arrives there with the divine sparks whole and then splits them off again to experience the divine glory of the Central Core, gathers them up after that to go back out into the outer space levels and releases them again to serve as teachers. This is when they remain on their own. The Oversoul then is free to produce another group of children as He has raised His last group of children well and trained them to take their place in the Creator's worlds.

Chapter Four

THE DEVELOPMENT OF OUR GALAXY

I approached the young man behind the counter of the gift shop at Kitt Peak in Arizona and asked, "Do you have a book that shows a picture of the star, Norma?"

"Do you mean the constellation Norma," he asked?

"I didn't know it was a constellation," I said. "I've seen it on August sky maps in astronomy magazines and thought it was a star."

"It's actually a constellation in one of the spiral arms of our galaxy," he answered.

Norma and Neil at Kitt Peak in Arizona

Neil and I had come early for a nighttime program at Kitt Peak during the time when the comet Hale-Bopp was at its brightest. This gave us time to look around and see most everything.

We had just finished eating a box lunch provided as

part of the program and were waiting for everyone to be issued binoculars before going outside to view the comet. It was very cold out with a fierce wind blowing. We couldn't stay out very long. Then we went into the observation building where I thought we would be warmer. Little did I know that they would open the whole top of the building exposing us to that same cold wind, but it was worth it. There were about twenty of us in the group when we started but it quickly narrowed down to about ten or twelve because of the cold.

We saw many things including a galaxy I believe they said was 55 million years old. We saw twin stars, we saw the polar cap on Mars, but the most impressive things were the galaxies, the Sombrero galaxy was one, but also others in the spiral shape which our own galaxy has.

"You know," I said to Neil, "these spiral galaxies remind me of the picture of the whirlpool you took at Niagara Falls a couple of years ago. I'm also reminded of galaxies when they show radar pictures of hurricanes on TV. I guess it's the same motion whether its water, clouds or a sea of stars. They all end up in a whirlpool motion if the conditions are right."

"Let's use our imagination and pretend that we can get into a stream of whirling stardust and get on the TimeTraveler's magic carpet," I said. "He can take us to the TimeSpot on the TimeLine of Eternity that will allow us insight into the process that took place to form our Milky Way Galaxy."

The Milky Way Galaxy

From the beginning when the energy started attracting other swirls of energy in outer space, it was master-minded by the first Mind, the Divine Mind. The plan was laid out for eons to come.

The energy of this Mind has always been. It is and was sustained by clouds of subatomic particles whirling in from the far reaches of time and space or eternity as we call it. These clouds of particles split apart as they neared the central ball of energy, and the intelligent pieces of matter gravitated to the core.

These pieces of matter had programmed into them information as to how the universe would proceed to be formed. It's like instinct in animals. They all knew their part in the eternal plan of a perfect universe for the perfect energy of the Creator to abide in. It was determined by these particles just how long each stage of man's evolution would last and how each spinning top of energy would split and form galaxies. As to who programmed the particles, it certainly was a mastermind, the Creator himself, an all-powerful, wise and forceful core of energy.

The Universe Compared to Whipped Cream Salad

Yes, there is a God, a powerful, all-pervading energy whose presence is everywhere in everything. It is an energy field filled with thoughts so potent they are dangerous in the wrong hands and used for the wrong purpose. It is all so complicated that one is at a loss as to how to pull it all together for explanation.

To explain God in a very simple manner, please picture a whipped cream fruit salad. God is the mixture in which all else takes place, the ingredient without which there would be nothing. Without the whipped cream as the holding ingredient, all parts of the salad would fall apart. The fruit are individual themselves in the whipped cream; they still retain their taste and characteristics, but without the whipped cream they have little relationship to each other, except for the fact that they are all fruit. God is the agent that bonds all together into a finished product.

At the bottom of the bowl, the energy (whipped cream) is bubbling and churning (picture a blender.) The different fruits are right on top of this bubbling and every so often an extremely strong bubble will be right under one piece of fruit, say a cherry or a grape. The bubble will propel this piece of fruit to the surface where it will float in one position (say the stem is up on the cherry) even though it is moving around the bowl, unless a strong bubble pops to the surface beside it. This will cause it to shift its position so the stem points a slightly different direction. It will stay afloat until the time when an extremely strong pull of suction from below will pull it under.

The bubbling at the bottom of the bowl, (spinning blades of the blender), is the center of God, the true center of our universe. We are like the pieces of fruit on the surface of the whipped cream going away from the bubbles. It is all an action of ebb and flow. We are never really away from God, because we are always in the whipped cream mixture.

When picturing the universe as a bowl of whipped cream salad the size of a football field, one should picture earth as one tiny cherry. See this football field inflated, as a football itself is and in the center visualize the bubble making machine. It is constantly at work; it never stops its action, so things it affects must always be changing.

If a picture were drawn of the universe thusly, there would be groups of fruit clumped together because one burst of bubbles shot them all to the surface at one time and this determines their floating position as they circulate around the football field. This is an action that is never sensed by one riding on the cherry because the clumps of fruit all stay in their same relationship to each other in their smaller cycles. A new burst of bubbles or even just one bubble can shift one of the pieces of fruit a slight bit and affect the others a slight bit.

In the whipped cream there are whirlpools formed by a spinning fruit, say a large peach, which pulls the smaller fruit into its whirlpool action and causes the smaller fruit to spin around the peach while they are all revolving around the football field. The exact nature of this bubble machine can be compared to the hydrogen atom that collapsed into the black hole.

The overall picture is one of the universe in constant motion. When a star sinks into a black hole (sucked under by a bubble in the whipped cream), it does not disintegrate to be no more. It simply waits with the rest of the bubbles to be popped to the surface again in a different time and place. When it does pop to the surface again, it must go through a cooling period. When it has cooled it starts the process of evolution all over again. There is no destruction of the stars, just appearances and disappearances. The football field sized universe with earth as a cherry and the sun as a peach, perhaps a grapefruit would be a better size comparison for the sun, are all part of the same solar system. There are many solar systems in our galaxy and there are many, many galaxies, each with many solar systems.

Energy Started Spinning

Perhaps you could picture a whirlpool as a rubber band spiraling downward. When it reaches a stop at the bottom, it will return, pull or spiral back, to the original shape. This is just one top, so to speak, that does this for one galaxy. There are many, many tops spinning, some at the beginning of the spin before the split, some having just split, some almost at rest and others starting the upward spiral. Does this give a better picture of what's going on out there? The process of evolution must be completed by all in one galaxy before the spiral can completely return to its beginning.

In the beginning the energy started spinning like a whirlpool and then, as the center got lower and lower, it split in half. The upper part of the whirlpool of energy stayed up and the bottom stayed down and is now in the process of evolving back up to the higher part to reunite. When the split occurred and energy sparks shot off the whirlpool, they fell after the lower half.

As the split apart took place (picture taffy spinning at a high rate of speed) pieces at the point of the break started breaking off and flying in all directions. This explains that the universe is still moving outward. These pieces have not yet lost their momentum. This is what is meant by the expanding universe. When they finally do lose their speed, they will drift to a stop. That will be the point where the universe stops expanding. This also relates to humans in that the energy that stayed up is the higher self, and what split off and dropped is the lower self. The sparks are the spirit that is evolving, bringing the lower and higher back to reunite. This is creation applied to humanity. The first ones to make the trip back up necessarily made it easier for the ones following, because the first ones blazed the path.

The point at which each receives the Godhead (the higher energy), where it can be given more help, is at the same spot where the initial break occurred, because this is where the higher energy is still waiting. When reunited with the upper broken end, the rest of the spiral upward will be much faster and easier. Earth is almost there at the point of the break. There will necessarily be a bump or jolt when they reunite and all the dirt and dust of her travel that she collected on the spiral down and on the path of return to that point must be gotten rid of. This occurs as the planet reunites with the broken end of the higher part, the Godhead, the head of the spinning top. This will be the move of the planet into its new orbit. It has to swing inside the Godhead.

The Godhead Compared to an Artesian Well

As a simple explanation of the Godhead, picture an artesian well, ever flowing sweet, pure water, very deep and refreshing. Picture a bare desert where this well is suddenly and miraculously set down in the middle of it. This desert is eternity, deep, dark, utter emptiness and blackness. (Eternity and time and space are all one.) This barren desert now begins to blossom and bloom with the water from the well. If this water source is removed, all will dry up and disappear again. This is what happens to planets if the Godhead is removed from them. As you know, there can be some growth in even the most barren of deserts. Planet earth is swinging into the Aquarian Age, which is the water sign. The Godhead will release the water from the artesian well, and earth will become a sacred planet.

This dry desert that we're discussing can be likened to humanity without the truth about its origins. As stated, a little growth can take place under these conditions, but very little progress will be made. Once humanity has the truth, spiritual progress will be phenomenal. This cannot take place until earth becomes a sacred planet. This is what is meant by the phrase "the living well-spring of water," or "the stream of living water" that has been talked about throughout the centuries, but is not understood. It is very difficult to understand. It is like a belt of energy that completely fits around the earth. Not a belt exactly, but like one balloon inside another. It is above the atmosphere of the earth all over the earth's surface, or will be when the earth shifts on its axis. That will swing the smaller balloon (earth) completely inside the larger balloon (Godhead) and earth will then be a sacred planet. It is like the reverse action of a baby being born. The baby has been encased in a bag of water which is broken and the babe expelled. Picture this action in reverse, like running a film backwards and you'll get a better idea.

There are many planets in the universe as a whole. Some are in dry desert stages, not having their turn yet to receive help and guidance from the Godhead. Some have had their turn and are already sacred planets. Earth is unique in that she is the only one at this particular stage of evolution at this time and therefore is a matter of great interest to all the close inhabited planets and to a few very distant ones.

The evolution of other stars has progressed so far beyond us that they are pure energy now. This energy is part of the Godhead that will encase the planet – energy of living thoughts and ideas. It will be available to tap into for guidance in the coming new times. That is why we will enter an age of peace and prosperity – because of this guidance. It is getting closer all the time.

Spirit Mind Caught in Swirling Energy

The principle of "like attracts like" had come into play and the galaxies, stars, suns and planets were being formed. At the same time, the part of the spirit mind that was caught and swirling around in this process was given birth as the mind of our Oversoul. This was when Michael, our Creator God was born. He watched as our galaxy, the Milky Way, as we call it, came into being. He, as the Oversoul of our galaxy, will use it to gain His own spiritual growth.

All the solar systems are afloat in their own "galaxy" or "sea of energy" that surrounds each individual stream off of the nuclear explosion that took place with original creation. Each ray or streamer makes up its own solar system; therefore, each solar system had a birth similar to the original. This birth for our galaxy, the Milky Way Galaxy, was the Great Central Sun (physical body) or Christ Michael (spiritual body). This was His beginning.

Actually, our galaxy came into being as an accident because of the implosion of matter that had created itself through an eternity of energy, positive and negative attracted together. Each universe eventually implodes into this tiny black hole and explodes back up again, completely rejuvenated; the same process as with planets, the same process with humans, until perfection is reached. Then the universes no longer implode; they expand and move outward and continue becoming more glorious and truly divine, as do planets and as do humans.

A nuclear explosion being a "chain" reaction means that the same process of buildup and explosion happened repeatedly in many different directions – like the rays coming off the sun. We are still in the chain reaction from the original explosion. It is still going on. Picture it as being in slow motion. The changing and forming of new planets and suns and stars is the continuation of the original nuclear explosion. But the continuation of the chain reaction will be stopped if the second stage of the nuclear explosion takes place on the earth plane. In other words, what our scientists do will affect our whole solar system. Our atomic bomb was not quite accurate in the splitting of the atom. Therefore, the second stage of the explosion was not reached. This is what saved our planet from annihilation and also allowed the continuation of the rest of the galaxy.

The reuniting of the two droplets as described in the second chapter is the clue. Our scientists left them split, which was the first part, the implosion. If the two droplets had joined when the energy rushed back in this would have brought about the second stage. Had our scientists achieved this second stage, it would have stopped the chain reaction of the galaxy and suspended all growth. All matter bodies would have stopped developing at the point where they are now. Our planet would have been destroyed and all else put into suspended animation in a frozen stream of time. This would have harmed the Creator, the central core of energy, because our galaxy is a streamer off from Him, remember. The way to make this second stage happen will not be divulged to anyone ever.

At the time of the original explosion there went forth twelve rays or "chains" of energy that all went through the same process of buildup and explosion before settling into their place in the seventh universe. This time the twelve streamers all had twelve differentiations of frequency. These twelve streamers are the galaxies, remember, and each galaxy gave birth to twelve solar systems. Our solar system is based on a pattern of twelve different "states of being" as far as frequencies. Each of these twelve different frequencies relate to a tone of the musical chromatic scale. The universe is alive with musical vibration at all levels in all space continuums.

In our universe there are time tubes that run through the universe which, when found, would make space travel much easier and faster. The vibratory rate within these time tubes is totally different than the vibratory rate outside the tubes. Inside the tubes the rate is tightened up. This is not the same as speeded up. There is a big difference. To speed up the vibratory rate makes a shimmer effect. To tighten the vibratory rate means to pull it together and make it sharper. Speeding up diffuses it; tightening it sharpens it. It is the same identical vibratory rate that is outside the tubes but is tightened, which reduces the distance. This is quite difficult to describe to those who have no concept of the makeup of this vibratory rate.

Time Tubes Compared to Rice

The closest thing that can be given as an analogy would be to picture a field of cooked rice as the outside of the tube and a field of uncooked rice as inside the tube. The field of cooked rice spreads out over a more vast area with the same amount of rice that would make up the inside of the tube. Since the original measurement of the rice was identical you would be using the same amount of vibratory rate in both areas only you could travel through it much faster as uncooked rice.

These tubes are areas or tunnels or sacs in which the vibratory rate has not been able to spread out in the vastness of space. They are original tunnels of the original vibratory rate at the moment of the big bang, the original nuclear explosion. Therefore, they are pure and clean and are welded together in a frozen stream of time. These tunnels can never be gotten rid of. They are as though you took a hard surface and glued the uncooked rice to it. Picture a field with a path of uncooked rice through the middle of it. Say it took a pickup truck load of uncooked rice glued in a single layer to make a path across this field a couple of feet wide. The same pickup truck load of rice, the same amount, is cooked and piled beside the path (that has high walls so it cannot have any uncooked rice spread into it). The cooked rice begins to spread out on both sides of the path and eventually covers an area a hundred times larger than the path through the middle.

If you were traveling and your travel was based on grains of rice instead of miles, you can easily see how much quicker you would get to your destination by taking the path through the middle. Each grain of rice, each mile of space, expands to approximately one hundred times the original.

Force Field of Galaxy Contains Mind

The coming together of two giant star nebulae was the mating of a sun higher than our Central Sun, as we term it, and resulted in the "mind" of Christ Michael and also His physical body, the Central Sun. The mind of Christ Michael is the force field of the Milky Way galaxy spoken of as the Oversoul.

The result of this mating is the original feeling of love between the male and female aspects of Christ Michael that are circling the galaxy. But the part that held the original feeling of love has separated from the main force field and is a circling cloud of gas. It circles faster than the large galaxy it separated from and also faster than the physical body of the sun. Every five hundred years it approaches close to earth and the ripples pulse every four years. This gaseous cloud does have a name that is known to our scientists. Its universal name is Libely; its earth name is Libra.

The same as we could send out over the ethers a thought of love in a circle, so also does the Great Central Sun, Christ Michael. It is a very special aspect of Him. His thoughts of all kinds are in the great Milky Way force field, but this much smaller gaseous cloud (Libra) has the original feeling that took place at the moment of ecstasy at the mating between male and female. It is embedded in all on earth, all kingdoms, as the kundalini, the root chakra. If one is open to it they will be quite sensitive to this feeling the next time Libra cycles near us. How they use or interpret this sensitivity is their decision. They can attach feelings of emotion to it, or absorb it into writings or music, or some other form of creativity, perhaps lecturing. The choice is theirs; it is there for all to use.

As given, it is closer every four years and very, very close every five hundred years, due to certain rhythmic impulses of the universe. All the stars in the zodiac have embedded in them or surrounding them, a certain part of Christ Michael's make-up – His emotional make-up – such as anger, strength, joy, love, etc.

This cloud actually is the crossing of the paths of two giant star nebulae that both have concentrated amounts of the Christ Consciousness thought-forms in them. One is male, one female and when they cross paths or "mate," so to speak, they give off an emanation of Christ love that fills the solar system. Anyone that is in tune will hear the message, as it is broadcast to all areas of the Milky Way Galaxy.

The path of progress of this force field is charted and kept track of. It is stronger at regular cycles of five hundred years. At other times what you get is more of a reflection or bouncing or echoing. It is like ripples or waves on a pond that grow stronger with each pass of a boat that is circling the pond. The ripples start dying down until the boat comes back around again when the ripples turn to waves, to again dwindle away until the boat passes again.

Twin Stars Compared to Humans and Cookies

The Great Central Sun is part of a triplet star. The left hand separation is in a different galaxy. Both the middle, which is our Great Central Sun, and the right hand side, its twin, are in our galaxy. The right hand side does not have any in orbit around it yet as there are only three solar systems completely formed in our galaxy thus far although there will eventually be twelve. This is not an ordinary triplet; it was one nebula that split and then one half of it split again.

The Great Central Sun is one half of the half that split. For this reason it is not a true member of a set of triplets. It is closer to the half it split from, but at the same time it is closer than any other to the first half that did not split.

For the moment let's disregard this first large original half of the nebulae and discuss the second half that split again. As given, one half of this is the Great Central Sun in our galaxy. Its twin half is also in our galaxy; the large original part that split is in a different galaxy. I will call them sun #1, #2 and #3. #1 and #2 are the original split halves with #1 being in a different galaxy and #2 being the Great Central Sun in our galaxy which then also split. The other half of the split, #3, is also in our galaxy awaiting it's time to form its own solar system. For the time being it is inactive as far as attracting any other bodies in space to it.

What makes a binary twin is the splitting of the nuclei at the absolutely correct moment when the star is in the formative stage. The exact same thing must happen with a human fetus to produce an identical twin. The splitting of the cell must happen at exactly the right time for both to survive. There are many instances where a cell may split but it is either too early or too late for an exact carbon copy to be produced.

The same thing holds true in the big universe. The state of the gases in the nebulae must be the exact correct temperature and the speed of revolutions must be absolutely correct for a clone of the star being formed to be produced.

When the split occurs, this will be when conditions are right for a "mirror" image to be drawn off the opposite side of the forming star.

The same thing takes place with a human fetus. The formation of cells must be exactly right that all organs will be mature enough to be able to produce a clone. What can happen if the split takes place too late is what we call Siamese twins. The split came perhaps a few hours too late and one organ or perhaps two or even three were past the time when they could clone themselves. All other parts of the fetus were able to produce a clone except, say perhaps, the kidney or the liver and the two fetuses share this one organ. Sometimes all the organs are able to clone but the timing was so close that the final withdrawing apart does not have time to take place. The only connection between them is tissue between the chest wall and perhaps the wall of the stomach. It is a simple matter, then, to finish this separation. It is not so simple in other cases.

Picture in your mind two cookies that were placed too close together when put on the pan to be baked. Where they touch it is a simple matter to cut them apart. If they are only partially cooked and you could pick them up and pull them apart, there would be an ungainly bump in the outside symmetry of the cookie at the exact spot where they separated.

The same thing will be true of binary stars. There will be an ungainly bump in the otherwise symmetrical outline of these stars. The bump will be on opposite sides as they would be on the opposite sides of the cookies, if you had marked them with north and south polarities.

These non-symmetrical occlusions in the outside of the stars will be the clue to establishing binary twin stars. There will be a way to determine these occlusions. This will be by a concentration of certain prominent gases at this particular spot. Say, for instance, in our cookie example there were dabs of chocolate on top of the cookie that, of course, melt as the cookie bakes. If you were to pull the cookie apart while the chocolate was in this melted state, the chocolate would have a tendency to run to the center of the area between the two cookies as you picked them up and pulled them apart. The chocolate would be stretched, then, at the very outer edge of the break. Therefore, you would have not only a concentration of chocolate at the spot of breakage, but you would also have a stretched area of this chocolate at the very break. This could be applied to the process of determining which ones are binary stars.

Other factors to look for would be size, which will not be exactly the same. Not even in the case of identical twins on the earth, whose cells split at the absolutely correct time, will their sizes be exact. They will be close, but you could not demand that stars be the exact height and weight and circumference to be classed as identical twins. You would never have any in this classification if this were the requirements.

Therefore, the binary stars will not be the exact same size. This would come closer to being true in a triple star separation or in the case of humans, a set of triplets. There would most always be two of the three that were the exact same size and one that was not. The reasons for this phenomenon are extenuating in both cases and don't need to be gone into at this time.

The makeup of the stars will not be exact either. In the process of cloning a star, outside factors will influence the partial solidification of the star material. In other words, once they are freely apart from each other, drift will move them immediately further apart. They will be drawn to the nearest object of solidity. In the passage of movement they will pick up half formed or still forming bodies of smaller stars and these will be incorporated into their makeup. This is what will cause the difference in internal makeup.

This process of drifting apart is what is responsible for one half of the binary twin to be in one galaxy and the other half in a different galaxy. This drift has force behind it; the force of being pulled apart. Say you are pulling apart two cookies that separated except for a center section. These are tough cookies and you have to pull quite hard to finish separating them. As your hands fly apart when the cookies are free of each other, one hand will go to the right and the other to the left. Say you have two different plates of cookies sitting on the counter one to each side of you. You would drop the cookie in the right hand on that plate and the cookie in the left hand on that plate. One plate of cookies is sent to a neighbor next door for a holiday treat. The other plate is boxed up and sent across the ocean to where, perhaps, your son is in the military service in a foreign country. You must see the same thing happening to the binary stars in order to understand why one can be in a galaxy different from another. Also, one cookie could be analyzed in a lab experiment, the recipe determined and more cookies like it produced.

The other cookie could never be eaten, but also never be used to produce more of the same or attract more of the same. It would eventually become stale and harden and no longer be useful.

This is what happened to our central sun's binary star. It was never eaten, nor was it analyzed so it could attract other cookies to it. It is a lonely star in another galaxy and is serving no particular purpose at this time. Its makeup internally is very, very similar to our sun, but it has not attracted any planets into orbit around it due to its location in the universe. Its live qualities did not readily attract any star near it. It was moving faster than our sun and that caused it to not be able to cement an attraction.

Our half of the binary star was born in the approximate area it is in at the present moment. In other words, one of the baker's hands was pulling harder than the other. Our half of the cookie stayed pretty much where it was, but the other half moved with much speed through the universe not attracting anything to it.

This other half could hold planets in orbit if it could attract any, but the attraction process must take place at exactly the right time also. This could be compared to a female of the animal species attracting the male at the right time.

Communication Network like Telephone System

There is a network of communication among three solar systems and also a separate network between most planets in one solar system. The intricate workings of our telephone communication system may be a good comparison to the communication network of the galaxies. The universe is so large, it is unfathomable. It frightens people to picture it this way, but they really need to be able to see and believe this. It should not make anyone feel useless or unneeded as all are part of energy lines and without them these energy lines are shorted out. This is why each spirit on each planet in each galaxy is vitally important to the overall energy line. They must all light up, so to speak, or that particular line of communication is dead until they do. Eventually they will. Picture each divine spark as a fiber that should glow in a fiber optic light. They are all needed for the beauty of the lamp to be complete. This is what is holding earth back from plugging into this network of communication through its energy line. She must become a sacred planet and be connected with the others by each divine spark taking its rightful place. This is very confusing and difficult to explain to those who have no concept of the overall purpose or plan for the universe as a whole, because it is such an immense picture.

You are a thought-form of energy, spun off that Oversoul, who progresses through twelve planes of inner life, which is mimicking the outer life (you), who is mimicking the Oversoul, who is mimicking the central core or God. You are the reality you at this given moment, and all others are the reality you on lower and higher levels. You can expand your universe by adding more mirrors to look into and extending the tunnel or channel. Your soul is a child of the Oversoul, who is a child of the central core or God, the same way your probable realities are related to you.

There is no end or beginning of time or space. It is all one huge sphere. Your path is laid out and can be seen for a certain stretch until it goes over the horizon. A certain part of it can be seen by those who are sensitive. A lot that happens to individuals cannot be changed, but some of it can be altered as these are lessons presented as your opportunities to grow and you have the free will to decide if you choose to learn the lessons this time or not. The ones that cannot be altered were set up by your teachers. They were stubbornly telling you that you can't put them off any longer. You are going to learn them this time. You always were and always will be the entity that you are now.

The particles in your brain are your genes, pre-programmed with certain traits as the particles in the universe are pre-programmed as to kingdoms. Genes are a combination of human family traits infiltrated with the incarnating entity's energy. They are mixed. The human traits are there, of course, at conception, but have to be energized by the incarnating entity. This is a combination of traits of the zodiac sign and the personality ray. The influences of energy of the planets at the time of birth are what infiltrate the genes already present in the baby.

Comparing Humans to the Large Universe

One should compare one's self to the universe and the universe to one's self. Your mind must be considered a sphere of solid time and space. The moon, though dead, is still in time and space. So are all the incarnations you have had also dead, but still in time and space. All you have been or will be is programmed into your core or inner seed, as were the particles that feed the mastermind of the universe. These particles (genes) feed the inner core of you. They are programmed to act and react a certain way. That is why it is said that much coming at you cannot be changed.

You are (like the galaxies) constantly trying to bring your lower self and higher self together into a balanced whole. The living stream of water, the Godhead, is in your mind and when the lower self is raised to meet the higher, you can tap into it for much help and guidance in all areas. This is the universal mind or as explained about the universe, the Godhead.

The pass through the Oversoul, the Milky Way Galaxy that our solar system revolves through accounts for periods of great spiritual strides forward that humanity has taken and for masses of people to "open up" to their inner (esoteric) self. This is the start of the fourth pass through the Oversoul. As people "open up" to assimilate these more powerful vibrations, they raise their own vibrations to their higher etheric selves and contact the real fourth dimension on the etheric level of the planet.

They retain its beauty and color and high vibratory rate as they bring it into existence, then, on the earth plane, the exoteric plane. The unmanifested plane is the esoteric (spiritual). The manifested plane is the exoteric (physical). Both are etheric matter (divine) just a difference in vibratory rate.

Humanity must parallel events in the universe. It can be no other way. Once you have done this, your life can never be the same. It should become much more fulfilled. You must live according to the dictates of your higher self, never your lower, or you will lose this achievement. Listen to what it is telling you. It comprises your universe. If not following it, you feel like a star that has gone wild, out of its natural orbit and most likely headed for disaster. It is very complicated to compare your mind to the universe but as above, so below. As the universe comes to a stop, your mind will have expanded to total capacity, far beyond the ten or fifteen per cent now used. As each star must help other stars evolve, so must you help all those you are associated with as they are part of your universe.

The upheaval that is gone through prior to balancing or joining of the two selves is compared to the upheaval earth will experience when it moves into its new orbit. It must have a new beginning and it must be built in the mind. So must a new beginning be built for an entity who has joined the two selves. It also must be built in the mind through transmuting attitudes. This must be stressed. This is why early education is so important. All the minds of children are universes making up one huge universe. These explanations given here are vital to helping others understand that the Kingdom of God is within.

The three bodies, physical, emotional and mental, are, of course, inside you. They are the kingdoms, so to speak, of your universe. The physical body is of course easily understood. The emotional is next easiest, but the mental body is tricky to really understand. The mental body is the mind of your probable realities (other incarnations) plus your present mind and the universal mind. The mental body is not functioning in most humanity, or rather only one third of it is. The person's own mind is all that is working in most. Therefore, the mental body is usually overpowered by both the physical and the emotional bodies. If the physical body says it doesn't feel well or is too tired, the mental body lets the physical get away with it. The same thing happens with the emotional body. The emotional body will affect the physical and the mental body is just too weak to do anything about it at all.

You can readily see how the transmuting of bad attitudes is the only way to strengthen the mental body, so it can start having some influence on the other two. This is really what was meant by the trinity, as the mental body is the place where the divine spirit is.

The really intelligent part of humanity can readily understand these concepts, but the majority, especially older individuals, will have a very difficult time with them. This is why education in the future must focus on attitudes.

All Have Twelve Levels of Progress

Our galaxy had the same beginning as all life in the universe. Humanity all has the same Oversoul, Michael, the Creator God, so all are tied together this way. The

Oversoul has His twelve levels (planets) of each solar system. Each individual soul on earth has his twelve levels of each planet (twelve levels for each of twelve mind dimensions) to evolve through. The Oversoul must evolve through the twelve planets, which are the planes of progress for Him, before He can exit this solar system. The galaxies are in order. The gaseous cloud of dust that forms solar systems, that will form the next one, is already forming and can be detected by our astronomers. It really is mind-boggling, isn't it? The minds of these new bodies will be those who never descended onto a star or planet because their bodies haven't formed yet and are in the process of formation now.

Chapter Five

THE BIRTH OF OUR SOLAR SYSTEM

We were visiting my sister who lived just a mile and a half from Saguaro National Park outside Tucson, AZ. We had been coming here for many years to see my mother, stepfather and brother before my sister moved here, but had never before taken the time to see the Visitor's Center.

"Wow, look at that sunset," Neil said as we came out of the Visitor's Center.

"Isn't it beautiful?" I replied. "If you have your camera and tripod with you why don't you take a picture?"

Cactus in Moonlight

"It can't turn out any worse than the pictures I took of the moon the other night," answered Neil, laughing.

This was one of Neil's biggest failures – trying to get a picture of the full moon with the cactus. But he was still learning and experimenting.

"You really are much better at taking pictures of the sun than you are at taking them of the moon. I'm always amazed at the differences in sunsets taken in different places. Can you imagine what it must have looked like when the sun was first forming?" I asked.

"It would have been so brilliant that no one in a physical body would have been able to look at it," Neil responded.

"You're probably right. Wouldn't it be great if we could experience that event with the help of the TimeTraveler?" I asked. "For a moment let's pretend that we can see the forming of the solar system. Let's follow the TimeTraveler as he takes us on another incredible journey and allows us to experience this. Let's ride the Carpet of Time with him and using our imagination glide up one of the rays of the sun and follow it back to its beginning."

Michael is Creator God Over Our Solar System

Our solar system had its start with the birth of the Great Central Sun, Oversoul Michael. As each piece of energy moved away from the birth hole (the main Creator or hydrogen atom), it was composed of fiery gases. Mixed with those fiery gases was the spirit mind. As each one of these pieces of energy moved out away from the womb of creation, there were spirit thought-forms swirling in with the gases with tiny filaments of thread still attached to them. These tiny filaments, the umbilical cords, are composed of ethereal matter

Michael Describes His Birth

It is I who see all. I could describe myself to you as a giant cloud of swirling energies that is high above your planet. I am the energy center for this universe. I do not deal in micro-man problems and destinies. I deal in macro-man visions and foresight. I see what is needed from a viewpoint that none can see, but am not even aware personally of different races, different religions or different opinions. These are left to my helpers of which there are legions.

The space was empty until the swirling cloud nebulae of which I was a part started forming into a solid mass. I deemed it wise to not get caught at that time in the swirling gases, but to stand above, separate for that instant in time, to watch and see what came of the tempest. It would be similar to you watching the forming of a new community being brought into existence from the barren ground up to a livable city before deciding to make it your home. I watched fascinated and excited as the Central Sun hardened into a solid, forming my physical body.

The universe is filled with beautiful suns everywhere. We did all come from out of a black hole as a bubble popping up from the central core. As we came up into an atmosphere different from the dark warmth of the womb of creation, we were frightened at first, wondering where we

were and why we were there and what we were to do with ourselves. It seemed to be instinct to stay close to our birthplace; in fact, we were still getting nourishment from the central core through the birth passage of the black hole of birth. So we continued to swirl around getting braver all the time and joining with other bits of clouds and then inviting gases to mingle and intermix with us and we detected the formation of a central core.

When the birth hole eventually sealed over and healed, we were on our own, ready at last to take upon ourselves our destiny, that of becoming a beautiful child of the Creator who gave birth to us from the center of His being, that central core of the universe, an atom so small that none can detect it, but feel its energy we do.

The virtues in my makeup each have a different vibration that all joined and provided a beautiful melody that accompanied the birth of each planet as it whirled and swirled and separated itself from me, the Central Sun. I continued to watch the gasses and clouds separate into the hardened forms of the planets. I am the Oversoul. I know how each planet came into being and what part of my many components made up the central core of each of them.

Birth of Sun Compared to Birth of a Baby

At approximately five billion years ago, the events taking place were the formation of our sun and the birth of the planets in our solar system. When our sun was born, the first part of the fireball to rise out of the black hole was a powerful cloud of gas, similar to the sac of water that is broken and released when a babe is born. This fluid is a vital part of the babe that has served its purpose and enters the creative system again by being eliminated and returned to nature. This is an extension of the process that is going on internally in the body of the mother. In our analogy, instead of water this was gas that extended off the sun. This gas carried with it subatomic particles. Actually, it was made up of subatomic particles. It was an extension of the process being carried on in the core of the sun, the process of birth.

When our sun first was born, coming up out of the black womb, the black hole of birth, its light was so brilliant; its energy was so strong, that it destroyed all that came within a close distance by pulling them into its fireball. It took a certain amount of time for it to cool enough that those attracted to it fell into their gravity pattern and stayed in set revolution around the sun. When it was first born, with the intensity of the heat and energy coming off of it, our planet could not have been as close as it is now without being engulfed by it. This sun did attract many and gobbled them up, so to speak, before it calmed its force field down enough that the planets that were attracted to it weren't destroyed. That attraction period is still in effect, holding the planets in their orbits around this sun, and will be in effect for a while longer.

Birth of the Planets

To begin with, the energy was a cloud of whirling gases. The cloud of whirling gases broke into many different size clouds of gas. The next stage was the phenomenon of "like attracts like" which led to the grouping together of gases and bits of congealing nebulae into all those of like mind. The next stage was the attraction by properties of frequency. This was followed by a grouping together into bodies of half-formed stars. These half-formed stars grouped into constellations, the constellations, then, were the means of forming planets capable of life. Each constellation "pooled" its resources of thought-forms and "gave birth" to a planet, or perhaps even twin or triplet planets.

Twelve Planets in Solar System

Twelve progressive planets make up our solar system. Our scientists have not considered the fact that planets move in and out of orbit around different suns. The planet Orion was, millions of years ago, in orbit around our sun. The planet of Sirion will be pulled in when the new universe comes moving in. This new eighth universe is going to push Sirion into orbiting our sun. As Orion has moved out of our sun's orbit, so will Placeda move out. When it does is when Sirion will be pulled in. There must be a pathway of twelve progressive planets in each solar system. The astronomers in the capitol of our superuniverse see the pattern of the solar systems and universes shaping up long before it happens. They know this is planned and therefore have included it in the path of progress for our solar system. Some of these planets we have never heard of and some of the ones we do know of are not inhabited.

Planets Congealed Over Black Hole

The planets were nebulous puffs of air in the beginning. They did not so much rise up from a black hole as they congealed at the opening of the black hole. They started cooling and forming a protective case around the central part that was directly over the birth hole. The center of this core or shell was filled with the most liquid and fiery of the gases. As they congealed over the black hole, this stopped the feeding of the nebulae from the vortex. It was being fed energy. As this energy supply stopped, each planet was then able to solidify.

The first planet to be born was Orion and its total atmosphere was comprised of what we call electricity on our planet, but this was very strong electricity, more of a shimmering of electrical light.

Picture, if you can, a bowl made up of clear crystal Jell-O. Each of the tiny little squares of Jell-O that make up the whole bowl of Jell-O have a lattice structure that not only ties it to the next one by magnetic attraction but also reflects the light produced by the friction of each little square of Jell-O rubbing against the next.

•This first planet was light, made up of this strong electricity. This electricity is still available on this first planet.

•The next planet found its atmosphere emitting an aura of powerful electricity. It was different than the form of gas we think of; it was "electrified gas."

•This electrified gas became mixed with carbon or ash and formed a gas in the form that we know gas to be in. Helium was the form of atmosphere on the third planet.

87

•This helium was split by electric charges as planet earth was brought into being. This combination of helium being shattered with electricity of a voltage so high we could not begin to understand it, produced hydrogen.

•The hydrogen of our planet combined with the solidifying and evolvement of the mineral kingdom, and produced neon gas.

•This combining took place in an orderly manner. The processes of evolution on each planet were incorporated into the atmosphere of the following planet and produced a different gas which then in turn "floated" in the solar system and changed the original atmosphere of all the planets. These are what we call the active gases

.

When the planets were first born, the friction of birth continued building as they exploded up out of the black hole. The friction from coming up out of the black hole caused them to grow and expand, similar to a human being who will continue to grow and expand in physical proportions until they have reached the teenage years or the early twenties perhaps.

Planets are exactly the same; the sun is exactly the same. They continue a proportionate amount of time, as the amount of time that the twenties took out of the human life. The same proportionate amount of time is taken out of the life of the sun to continue growing and expanding in physical proportions.

Now as the human continues to grow and expand mentally, spiritually and emotionally, so do the planets and the suns constantly grow, expand and evolve spiritually, but not in physical size. As the human body

88

begins its downward journey after reaching its peak, so do the planets and the sun. The physical form, once it has reached that peak, continues to deteriorate as the mind and the spiritual body continues to grow. There must come this separation stage. Humans call it death as it also is called for the planets – the death of a star.

The planets and sun were born out of black holes, outward bound vortices of the central core, but have access to their centers through mini-black holes, inward bound vortices into themselves. (For the purpose of explanation I refer to a black hole as an outward vortex of energy, and a mini-black hole as an inward or inverted vortex.)

The part that sealed over on planet earth (it can be compared to the navel in humans) was at the location on our maps at the spot where the isle of Crete is today. This has always been a place of easy entrance into or onto our planet for space ships, especially in the  early days of colonization. It would still be so.

More Communication from Michael

Yes, this communication is coming directly from the Oversoul. Does this surprise you? Who else could describe their own birth into the universe this way? I am a Spirit person, if you will; I am Michael, but I am not the Great Creator. I am the Creator of your planet and I gave your planet to my son Lucifer. I have other sons, Satania is one of them, but he is not the Satan referred to as evil – that is a different story. I am the Central Sun of your local universe, the Father of Lucifer. So, I am your Oversoul, but am not the Oversoul for most of the rest of the universes, just your particular solar system.

To explain further, our Oversoul Michael has twelve sons. When planet earth was born it came under the domain of Lucifer, our sun, the sun we see up in our sky. He, Lucifer, is the Oversoul of this planet earth and does have brothers – the other sons of Michael. At times Lucifer looks to the domains of his brothers for help and guidance.

Satania is Capital of Solar System

One of the other Michael sons is named Satania and the planet Satania is named for him. It is the capitol ruling world of our solar system and we actually know nothing of it. This capitol world of Satania is on the other side of the sun. It is a world constantly blocked from the view of those on earth.

The same sun that serves our world also serves the world of Satania. It is the connecting link of the total solar system, this sun of ours. This does make it difficult for those on Satania to direct the activities of planet earth because there is very seldom any contact with us. The only contact possible is by spaceships. They must go around the sun a certain distance until their transmitters can pick up the earth. This is where a large part of our UFOS are coming from. They are on missions sent out to enlighten the minds of those on earth that they are behind the rest of the solar system in their understanding of the solar system. Our scientists have not even forty percent of the knowledge of our total solar system. It is truly not totally our fault, because we cannot be in direct communication with those on the capitol of Satania.

Our sun spot activities interrupt all our radio transmissions from Satania at times and garble them. This is making it much harder at this particular time. There was a period several hundred years ago when contact with our planet was possible by those on Satania and some thoughts did get through, some transmissions managed to get through but were misinterpreted and this is where the term of Satan crept into our vocabulary. The message that we were one of Satan's worlds was misinterpreted. The last part of the word was lost and it became Satan's world.

It is Satania's world. It is under their jurisdiction. They are a planet approximately the same dimensions as ours and are approximately the same distance from our sun as we are, but they are higher beings. Not only does our sun block transmissions from them, it also blocks transmissions from higher worlds that are much easier for those on Satania to understand than for us. We do get some of this transmission, but not as clearly and as consistently and as much as they do. Therefore they have devised a system of space ships as stepping stones not only to them for transmitting purposes, but on up past them.

The duties of those inhabiting the capitol worlds of not only our solar system, but the other solar systems and local universes (galaxies), are in progressively higher stages of responsibility. The main duty of those on Satania is education. They are the final determiners of the continuation of the spiritual progress of any planet and of any on that planet in our solar system. It was they who determined that our planet was not ready for the fourth dimension. Their duties are to help us, their brothers and sisters on planet earth, learn, grow and evolve to the status required for the continuation of our journey. That journey will progress no faster than we ourselves dictate.

They are higher than the hierarchy. What is termed Shamballa is where the plans originate. The origin of Shamballa, the original Shamballa, is on Satania. They have a base on earth for their ships because they cannot continually go back and forth. They do not need to be in contact with their mother planet, because they know their duties; they know the plan. They do at times go home, if you will, to Satania for their rest and relaxation and take turns. Others will replace them, so there is probably what you would call a constant turnover of ships.

The word constant to them does not mean exactly what it means to us, because they have no time. Our picture of constant is a steady stream. When they say constant it could be twenty years, twenty-five or fifty. Time is a solid, if you wish to think of it that way. Think of it as a constant body of water – time, it's not going anywhere. It's there. They move in time, but time does not move them. Here again, this is almost impossible for us to realize. We are thoroughly ingrained with the changing seasons, the revolutions of the heavenly bodies, etc. They do not go by this. Their civilization is not on the surface of their planet, nor is Shamballa on the surface of our planet. Therefore, they are not affected by these tidal waves of revolution that tie us to time. The center of their sphere is their time, and as said, it's not going anywhere. It can't go anywhere as it is contained within the shell of their planet.

Planet Earth Most Difficult Planet

On Satania they talk of the "hell" that must be gone through on the earth plane. It is by far the hardest plane of existence and one cannot get out of it and progress on to better things until he "has shoveled coal into the fiery furnace" long enough to perfect and purify his own soul to the point of being able to progress on. Man does set his own pace and will stay in the turmoil of the earth plane either esoterically or exoterically, until he does his own purification. These ideas coming from the capitol world of Satania were tapped into at some point by some open channel communicator and were misinterpreted and only added to the confusion and wrong teachings of organized religion. As given previously, the name Satan was also a misinterpretation of Satania.

Sun is made up of Chemicals Needed for Life

Our sun, as our scientists know, is made up of many, many different kinds of gases. These gases have all the chemical elements in them to cause life to grow and flourish, not only on our planet but on all planets in our solar system. These chemicals can be pulled directly out of the sun's rays to do our healing, instead of manufacturing these chemicals into medicine. How to do this is quite advanced, but it is possible and in the future there will be equipment built that can do this. Then the bodies, the human forms, will be given an infusion of the chemical directly from our atmosphere, directly from our sun's rays. Our sun can provide anything necessary for the welfare and health and living of those under its care

.

Scientists Need to Look Behind Rays of Sun

Part of the problem of the way we are trying to use the exoteric energy of the sun on our planet is the fact that we are not reaching the married core, the wedded core, the positive and negative welded together. We need to get behind the obvious on the physical form of our sun to the deep inner part of the sun to reach its central core. In other words, scientists need to look past, look beyond, and look into the rays of light that this sun gives us. It's behind these rays that the goodness lies. The rays reflect so brightly, that they hide, blot out, or shield what is behind them, as far as our scientific equipment goes. So, to begin with, instead of trying to receive all the goodness from the rays of the sun, the equipment needs to be invented that will "part" the rays of the sun and let us in behind what appears to be where it all is coming from.

Our gamma rays, our X-rays, our solar energy rays, they're all good, but they're only the tip of the iceberg as far as reaching the depths of goodness our sun can give us. The gaseous quality of our sun can be harnessed, has been harnessed on higher planets, but it is not impossibility for our planet. This is the direction that healing must come from.

Sun Encircled by Rings of Vibratory Rate

The sun has many rings around it, many different vibratory rates in those rings, but those rings crisscross each other. They are not as the planet Saturn, where all the rings are in one layer, so to speak.

The sun is completely encircled or girded by these rings, twining around it in all different directions. Each of

94

these rings is made up of a specific chemical element. Because of the intense heat from the body of the sun itself, these chemicals are blended into the gases.

In other words, the ring closest to the sun can't get out through into the atmosphere uncontaminated or unblended with the other rings because it must come up through them. By the time that inner ring reaches through the outer it is a blending of all the rings – all the chemicals of each different ring are blended. This is what makes the gas that comes off from our sun, which then also makes up the rays which we receive from our sun.

Separating Machine Needed for Healing

There needs to be a separating machine. This machine is in practice on higher planets, it just has not been invented yet on our planet, but it is quite possible and not necessarily that difficult. It just is not known that it needs to be done; perhaps this will clue in some people to the point where they can accomplish this invention. When this machine is ready, this will then allow the gases to be separated into the different chemical elements. And it will just be, you might say, a matter of plugging into the channel of the separator that holds what we need for our body, either to heal or to keep in balance the health of our total body not just our physical body. The elements needed to keep our mental body and our emotional body plus the physical body in balance can all be retrieved from our sun if it is known how to do it. This will be the basis of a Healing Machine in the future. (The Healing Machine will be discussed further in the Science of Music, volume 10 of the notebooks.)

Goal of Sun was to Help Planets

The goal of our sun was to help the planets that were attracted to Him, those who fell into His magnetic pull and orbited around Him. To begin with, His goal was not to be an evolutionary planet for growth of evolving souls. This was not His goal. His goal was to help. Therefore, coded into His nucleus were the elements necessary for this sun to help these planets. As the sun's journey ends, as He fades and loses heat, then the bands are no longer being activated; they are no longer going to be needed as this sun's incarnation will be finished. These bands will shrink back in and become part of the hard barren core that is left and it will be eons before it goes back into the central core.

As the sun dies (and it has passed its brightest flare) and it continues to cool, these bands around it will solidify and eventually drop in, sink in and shrink in and become a part of the body of the sun, but the bands will no longer be alive with the elements at that time. The bands are energized from the heat of the sun. When this sun is on the inner planes to be rejuvenated, the bands are the means of injecting into the nucleus of this sun, all the elements needed to rejuvenate it.

The process is over a much longer period of time for the reincarnation of planets than it is for suns. Planets are a long time being born, they are a long time achieving the height of their incarnation and they are a long time on the downhill side. They linger in the ethers, in the state of suspended animation for a long time before they return to the central core to their inner planes. This is what many of the moons around the other planets are – the state that they are in. They have been energetic, life-

96

giving sources at some stage and in some gravity situation, not necessarily the one they are in at the present time. They have been attracted into the magnetic field of the ones they are around now, but weren't always necessarily there. Our astronomers have much to learn.

The Golden Age

The sun is a star that is cooling off. It is a huge star and as such will be a long time in the cooling down period. At the time of planet earth's birth, it (earth) was visible at all times for a long period of time also, as it was at the same stage then that the sun is in at the present time. There will be the birth of a new star that will replace the sun as it gets past the stage of giving light and warmth that it is now in, and another star in the solar system will take over the evolutionary track that earth has been used for. This will be at the end of the Golden Age of man when he finds the true God, the God Within.

The death of a star or planet is brought to pass by it forming a giant white star prior to death, which will be implosion into a black hole. This is the coming stage after the Golden Age of one thousand years when the mid-way point of earth's life is reached. At that time the down hill period which is becoming a white giant will start. Earth is still on the upward spiral out of the black hole of birth. When it is clear up out, there will be a pause of one thousand years before it grows so large it implodes and returns to its inner planes, the central core of the universe.

Our sun seems so cold, even though hot – so impersonal, so far away – yet it is the life giving force, the energy, for all on our planet. But our moon merely reflects the sun's light. It has no inner light of its own. Therefore, the rhythms of the moon have a different effect on the human psyche.

When we are turned away from the sun and do not receive its light being reflected from the moon, there is an entirely different vibratory pattern, or energy frequency, bearing on humanities' receivers in their animal brain, their energy receptors.

When we are in our dark stage – our night – and the moon is at its fullest at our particular spot in time, this energy that our receptors are receiving, a very weak reflected energy, has a strange effect on all things on our planet for that particular number of hours it is reflecting on us.

The moon itself is serving as a "movie screen," perhaps is the way to explain it – it's just serving to bounce that light off, so as the light hits the moon it doesn't receive anything from that moon – it's just bounced back to earth and therefore does not have any vitality. In fact, it has the ability to enhance any thought-forms in the path of the reflected light. Picture a movie projector and the dust motes that you can see that are enhanced in the beam of light from the projector to the screen. This is what happens from the screen that the moon is serving as, back that beam of light to our particular spot on earth. All thought-forms in that path are enhanced and most of them are our astral plane thought-forms which are not allowed to leave our earth because they are of not high enough quality.

This is why, when we are in our full moon stage, people have strange behavior patterns. It is also why it is easier at that particular time to reach the higher planes. If the receptor has cleared his own auric field, raised his vibratory rate high enough that the vibrations of these lower thought-forms are bounced off and only the high frequency ones are allowed through, then this one, at the full moon period, will have much better communication with the higher planes.

Twelve Stages of Solar System

We will have twelve levels in each of twelve planets to progress through – the Oversoul has twelve trips through twelve solar systems – all in the seventh superuniverse. Each planet has its twelve levels, each incarnation has its twelve levels, each year has its twelve levels, each school has its twelve levels, each pregnancy has twelve levels, nine inner and three outer. Yes this was not said before, but the spark has three months after birth to make a commitment to the physical form.

Path Compared to a Pane of Glass

Picture the Oversoul as a piece of glass that has shattered. Two little pieces (humans) can be found that fit together, but they still are a shattered fragment with rough edges that won't fit back into the whole until the right piece (twin soul) is found. This is the process that must take place before the piece of glass can be glued back together into one whole piece and then be moved into another room of the house that's being built. There are twelve rooms in this house and this piece of glass or window must progress from room to room. In some rooms it makes the move without incident, but in others it shatters upon arrival and must be pieced back together again before moving on. Each room is a classroom and each piece of glass learns through many lessons and much thought what it needs to learn, but at the same time it also needs to interact with the other pieces of glass, its brothers and sisters, if you will, that make up the rest of the sheet of glass. Getting to know others is a start in knowing all the shattered pieces of glass.

These fragments do have to be glued back together in the end and, I might add, eventually will be. In reality all pieces of the puzzle will eventually fit together. This is the lesson plan. The sharp edges of each need to be buffed off, smoothed up, so that they don't rub against another piece the wrong way and cause more shattering. If all edges get smoothed up, they will fit much better into the whole.

Now all this is an ongoing process. As each Oversoul moves out of the cycle of one solar system, another comes in. The new Oversoul has already started His trip through our solar system. There are always those in front of the group and a few of them entered in 1954 and a trickle of them since then. Most born from 1970 on are of the new Oversoul.

The Oversoul reincarnates in this solar system, as stated before, and the sparks entering bodies now are more highly evolved because they fell from a more highly evolved Oversoul. Our former incarnations were from a less evolved Oversoul, but still have many good qualities and knowledge and wisdom to help us. If you hear the third order being spoken of it is the Oversoul's third incarnation on planet earth.

Our past lives are still in time and space and so is the Oversoul's. We belong to the Oversoul's last trip. The Oversoul is getting ready to start a new trip, His fourth trip, through the solar system, a new order. When it is time for it to shower earth, earth must be ready to receive it, hence the step up in vibrations. The new incarnation of the Oversoul is of a higher vibrational rate. The energy waiting up above is the higher mind of the Oversoul.

Music of the Spheres

The extremely high frequencies of this energy are what is meant by the "music of the spheres." They can be heard by advanced instruments, but only the lower of the frequencies. Nothing yet is capable of registering the higher. If all could be heard at once, you would be able to hear the most beautiful harmony you could imagine, the harmony of the universe. In the future this harmony will be able to be heard and felt on a small scale and will be the way that is used to determine the state of health for all living things. The lower frequencies on earth's plane are distorting the harmony of the spheres, like a twelve string guitar with one string out of tune.

Our planet simply must be brought to the higher vibrational frequency. The timing element is all planned. Earth must move forward, ready or not, as a new planet is almost at the stage where the spiritual laggards of our planet will be sent. There can be a limited time overlap in the cycle, but not enough to throw the whole universe off. All proceeds in orderly fashion and ties back into itself. Because of the spherical shape of the universe, all must be placed according to a mathematical order or it would overlap. A belt worn around the waist must overlap to be buckled, but the universe cannot overlap or it would buckle. The planets are in order as far as the progression of life upon them goes. The different levels of different planes are really different planets. Planes, planets, it's the same thing.

Pass Through the Oversoul

When a "trip" or "pass" of the Oversoul is referred to it means each time He reaches a new plane and releases His children (thought forms). This is considered a "trip" or "pass." This is divine evolution. A root race pertains to physical evolution. The root race entering now is the sixth, and it is on the fourth planet as the third trip of the Oversoul. In other words this root race was released on planet four (earth) as an explosion of the third pass of the Oversoul. These root races are designations of thought-form experiments conducted by other planets. These were electrical thought-forms, rings of energy, if you will, from other planets. Another name for them is thought-adjusters. It worked the same way then as it does now only at a much lower level of evolution. Each time it took place was a step up on the ladder of evolution, well-planned by the Creator. It is well-planned still and ever will be.

The circle path is the over-all path for the divine sparks on each planet. They leave the Oversoul, go down and express in the "manner of life" that is the essence of each planet, following the planned path for completion of lessons for that planet, then back to the Oversoul and on to the next. The spiritual planets of progress (planes) are experienced on the physical bodies of the planets in our universe. The "Oversoul" being referred to is the thought-form embedded in the Milky Way Galaxy which is orbiting the solar system as we are, but at a very slow rate of speed. Earth has been moving with the Milky Way for as long as humanity remembers.

Our solar system cannot, will not stay in the form or shape our astronomers are wanting to lock it into. This is one of the biggest problem areas of misunderstanding as far as we humans go. We want everything to remain the same, unchanging forever. This can never be and the sooner this is realized and we learn to "go with the flow," the quicker will come understanding of our world, our solar system, our universe, our total journey, its goal and its new beginning. If all things stood still, if we never grew older, we would rot in our forms as we are now and that would be the end of our existence. We should worship our changing existence as it is our saving grace

Chapter Six

THE DEVELOPMENT OF OUR SOLAR SYSTEM

We were visiting the Getty Museum near where Neil lives in California.

"Hey Neil, can you get a picture of that bee getting pollen from the beautiful flower over there?" I asked."

"Yeah, let me try; I'll be able to as long as the bee holds still," Neil replied.

Neil and Norma at Getty Museum in California

"You know, the process of pollination that the bees carry out is the same process that brought our solar system to life. It's exactly the same, only instead of a bee, it was comets that brought life to the planets," I said.

"Pollination is a really important part of the Botanical Kingdom," Neil said.

"Yes, I've had several opportunities to realize that. I bought a bush for the front yard that had beautiful flowers on it when I got it and hasn't had any since then. I know it has something to do with pollination," I replied.

"If you're not afraid, why don't we pretend we can sit on the back of a bee which will magically turn into a comet and take us back in time to the TimeSpot where the TimeTraveler is waiting to show us how this all took place?" I said.

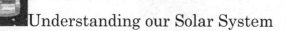

Understanding our Solar System

The creation story as written in the Bible is for planet earth. The Bible does not take into account any pre-existence to life on the earth plane. There was life on other planets for the divine sparks before they showered on earth. They had been on three previous planets and evolved through the processes on them. There has never been any breakthrough about this before. It is now time that these facts become known. It is necessary at this point in evolution. Compare it to schooling. A student must reach a certain level before certain subjects can be understood by him. We are finally ready to understand and need to be able to understand the complicated universe.

In order to give a more complete understanding of our Oversoul Michael, I will designate a difference between my use of the terms "flare" and "comet."

When the word comet is used it will mean a thought-form, which is invisible, (esoteric or inner).

When speaking of a flare it will mean a solar flare, or flare of fire, which

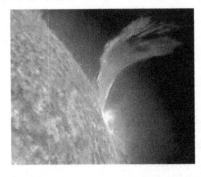

is visible (exoteric or outer). A comet (thought) travels through dimensions; it is not manifested. A flare does not travel through different dimensions. It is of physical matter. A comet (thought) can cross solar systems, galaxies and universes. A flare does not.

Sun's Name is Michael

Our Oversoul's name is Michael. He has brothers and sisters. Their names are not that important. You just need to know that all in the universe have brothers and sisters (using our language terms). Michael as seen by those on the planets is large and all-encompassing for all their wants and needs. He is totality for them in a way that nothing else can ever be. Without Him, they would not be. He is their total being, they are His total being. It is a marriage, if you will, between them.

Michael's capacity for love is endless, unlimited. It is almost inexpressible in human language as it is a feeling combining all virtues that must go into the making of a perfected being; compassion, kindness, intelligence, truth, impersonality, diplomacy and freedom.

Michael knows everything about the creation of the heavens and the planets – the nebulae forming into planets now, those planets no longer enriched with life forms. The term life-forms does not always include human beings. The life lived on the first three planets was not of the kind that can even be conceived of by humanity, but they did have an evolutionary plan like planet earth has. All three of the planets previous to earth had their plans and still have their plans. Yes, life of some form is found on all planets, but is not recognizable by us as life, because we have nothing with which to compare it. These early planet evolutionary chains are not appealing to us. The first one is simply air, that's all, just the atmosphere itself, but this is the start of life in our solar system – ions and neutrons that make up air, electrically charged air, that eventually starts forming into thoughts and ideas.

Beginning of Humanities' Spiritual Evolution

In the beginning of the universe there was vast emptiness, a void, nothing but black space, but you see, there is another universe beyond this one and explorers (a comet) from that universe invaded this black space and their momentum of traveling through it set up the motion that started the swirling of the energy that then started attracting and repelling and forming into groups and storms. (This is the very beginning of humanities' spiritual or esoteric evolution.) These explorers (the comet) passed through this empty black space close enough to the first planet to start the process of life on it.

The explorers or comet came from planet twelve of another universe on their way to another solar system. There was a spark of energy from that comet from another galaxy, a thought-form from the comet's galaxy that was part of the energy that washed planet number one Orion.

Process like Earth Plane Conception

The process can and should be compared to conception that takes place on the earth plane. When this spark of energy, this thought-form, impregnated the air on planet number one, it produced the  thought-form of humanity which then grew and grew and grew. It was a swirling mass of air and the thought subdivided and became so many different thoughts that it could not be contained on planet number one any longer. It was as though it had its incubation period on this planet and then it burst out of the womb of planet number one and proceeded to planet number two, Placeda, (Jupiter).

The thought-forms that started on Orion grew from a little tiny puff of air that was stirred into motion, remember, by the comet passing close by, the same comet that had awakened Michael. Until then this planet had been in what is termed suspended animation. When this comet got close enough that the energy waves from it washed ashore onto planet number one, Orion, these little tiny thought-forms of air formed; the subatomic particles started attracting and repelling. It grew to be quite a large, thinking mass of air. This is quite difficult for us to understand. This is the birth of Lucifer's mind, which you will soon see becomes the mind of all humanity when it shatters.

Flares are Atmospheric Disturbances Caused by Oversoul

The flares reinforce, or enhance, the effect of the "pass through the Oversoul." The Oversoul is the fact and the flare is the perpetrator of the act. In other words, the Oversoul, Michael, is the spiritual thought-form of concepts that are our goals. The flares from our sun (Lucifer) are the means by which we can reach the Oversoul's thought and accomplish our goals.

The first planet to harden and form was Orion and Michael, the Oversoul, wanted to experience it. When Orion passed through the force field of the Oversoul, the power and energy of the Oversoul of Michael caused the solar flare on Lucifer, our sun, which in turn caused the disturbances in the atmosphere of Orion. These disturbances then affected the energy thought-forms in the Oversoul. The flares keep coming, but they are still from the same Oversoul.

First Solar Flare – Demonia

As given, the first flare, Demonia came to planet number one, Orion, and interacted with the "first pass of the Oversoul." As a flare of energy it caused the air on the planet to join and mix and mingle with the Oversoul.

There was not much that this flare was capable of doing, only breathing air and blowing it around. This flare, Demonia, had a barren existence and did not accomplish much. All he could do was stay on planet number one as air until planet number two had hardened and formed enough that he could move to it. When this large thinking mass of air formed enough to ask, "Is this all there is," it immediately found itself on the second planet. Here it developed into small ringlets of atoms that make up storms – wind and rain. He, the first flare, Demonia, then continued this way, as air, through all the planets and went back into the body of Michael. Michael the Creator did not get much satisfaction out of that stage of experimentation.

Second Solar Flare – Harmonia

Michael then sent out another solar flare from Lucifer, our sun. The name of this flare was Harmonia. Harmonia intermixed with the Oversoul's "second pass" and caused separation into groups of harmonious thought-forms. This flare also went first to planet number one, experienced the same thing Demonia had, and passed on to planet number two, Placeda (Jupiter). Placeda was a little more advanced world. Here Harmonia watched her breath form into playful little ringlets of atoms, chasing each other around and enjoying themselves and having fun.

By this time Placeda was getting more of an atmosphere and a solid core to it and had more energy coming off from it – more sparking that caused Harmonia to separate and join into little thought-forms, little groups. Perhaps we could call them musical chords, or triads. But some had more than three in a group, you understand. There were all sizes of groups. Picture it as a big chorus in one area that all liked the same kind of music, say symphonic or classical music. The little group sitting over there on top of that mountain liked, say, spiritual music. There's a group of violinists back there in that little valley. There are all sorts of different groups with different instruments. This is planet number two, Placeda (Jupiter). Harmonia then left planet number two, moved through the rest of the planets and returned to Michael. Neither of these flares shattered into separated divine sparks. They experienced all as whole beings, whole flares.

Third Solar Flare – Satania

Only the third solar flare from Lucifer that Michael sent out succeeded in shattering and sending His children down as sparks to experience. This flare was called Satania, the third pass or trip of the Oversoul. He also went to planet number one, Orion. Planet number one was arid and barren of growth; perhaps I should say barren of nutrients. It was rock surface.

The Creator God, Michael, up there in the central sun didn't know what it was like to be down there on those planets, so He learned by having a tiny little filament of

111

thread stretching back to Him from all the solar flares coming off of Lucifer. From the first flare, Demonia, He learned to make thought-forms; on the second planet He had Harmonia, the second flare, set the pattern into musical groups because He, Michael, felt that after sending that first flare out and getting absolutely no return back through His filament thread, that maybe He'd better have some structure; some rhythm and harmony – some harmonious, mathematical structuring.

This was one of the concepts that He wanted to try out, so He set the pattern that when the flare moved to number two they formed into definite groupings of harmony.

Planet Number Two has More Stimulation

By the time Satania, the third flare, got to planet number two, Placeda, there was more nourishment, more interaction with more compounds in the soil, more minerals to feed this thought-form. This planet was not as barren as planet number one. There was no soil; there was just the beginning of sand crumbling off the rock surface. But here they were on planet number two with Satania, the third flare, and there was a lot of stimuli on this planet.

There began to be what you would term debates, perhaps. A group of thought-forms would join together here because they thought alike. Not exactly alike, but they all kind of agreed on several points. They continued forming into little rings, little bands of energy, little groups that saw things alike. Perhaps this group liked the atmosphere up on top of a certain point and another group thought perhaps the vibrations felt better to them at a different spot and this other group began to wonder if there was more to life than what they were seeing on this planet number two.

Unrest Begins

There was more on planet number two than there had been on planet number one, certainly, but not an awful lot more. The group that started wondering if there was more to life than this, started spreading the dissatisfaction, the unrest, to the others. The little storms started growing more agitated. Fights broke out and they knew they just couldn't stay there; they knew that planet number two could not contain them. They had grown. They just had to break out of the walls of planet number two. There just had to be something more. What an existence this was, just floating around there all day long, arguing with this guy, and arguing with that one. They couldn't even punch each other out because they were just thought-forms. There was a lot of mental debate going on, a lot of arguing back and forth about things

.

Groups Stay Together

The energy that forms into groups on planet number two tends to stay together through the whole trip. Eventually the groups get tired of playing around this way. Even though it is pleasant, it begins to seem quite useless. When this thought strikes this particular ringlet of energy, it leaves the atmosphere of planet number two and proceeds to planet number three.

Thought Forms Leave Planet Number Two

The storms grew bigger and bigger and they finally just left planet number two, "whoosh" in one huge cloud of energy. It was not in the form of fire or anything like that. It was still just like a cloud, only a big rolling, tumbling, turmoiling cloud. And it went to planet number three, which was Mars. The cloud was still in the gaseous form, but soon developed into a thinking bolt of lightning, an electrical line of energy.

Planet Three Not What was Expected

When the cloud of energy left planet number two Michael thought things would calm down on planet number three, that it would be a nice peaceful place to be and they could just go on with their concepts of what a perfect life would be. But planet number three was not what He expected. There was more anger, frustration, fighting and arguing.

This third solar flare from Lucifer, Satania, caused much more intermixing because it was a much stronger flare than the first two. (Eventually it came to rest on a planet of its own, Satania, which is the capital world of our galaxy.) Because of the anger and frustration this flare picked up on the planets as it passed through them, this flare got the reputation of evil.

Fourth Solar Flare – Persephonia

Demonia gave us the word demon, Harmonia gave us the word harmony and Satania gave us the word Satan. The next flare to come is named Persephonia and will give us the word perish. It is the cause of the vibrational disturbances felt at this time. The first flare was of a positive nature, male energy. The second flare was negative, female, energy and the third flare was, again, positive. The new flare is negative or female energy. Remember please, that these are the names of flares which are atmospheric disturbances. This flare will be stronger even than the third flare was and will intermix again with the Oversoul and will cause much upheaval and death on planet earth. But another meaning of Persephonia is "personification of revival of nature in spring."

When scientists realize the importance that atmosphere has on behavior they will be amazed and artificial environments will be initiated for humans to live in. The next flare after Persephonia will cause even more atmospheric disturbance and by this time, the only way life will be able to continue on earth will be in a protected environment.

Friction is the Spark of Life

Regardless, planet number three was causing much more friction than had been anticipated. There was something about it that just irritated  every one of the groups of thought-forms. The storms never did abate. They grew into massive storms and broke apart and formed numerous other storms which just kept growing and growing and growing. The friction became so tremendous between these thought-forms, these opposite factions of subatomic particles, that they finally started sending lightning bolts shooting off from themselves. This friction is the spark of life! It is the spark of life that is going to cause people to grow. If there is no friction there is no growth. There can be no growth without a catalyst.

Now remember what had been happening on planet number three? Remember all the frustration, anger and fights? We had gone from air to harmonious thought-forms to anger and frustration. To review, Michael, the Creator, had watched the thought-forms all the way from the first experimental world where all He did was breath air and blow that air around. He didn't get much satisfaction out of that world, that stage of experimentation, so He made a little more advanced world and blew that breath of air onto it. Here He watched His breath form into playful little ringlets of atoms, chasing each other around, enjoying themselves and having fun. He realized that if He made an even better world, these little ringlets could grow and expand, so He proceeded to do this

.

Third Solar Flare Satania Comes to Earth

What He didn't expect was that the conditions on this third little world would be such as to cause these little groups of atoms, these little puffs of His breath, to become angry and form into violent storms, with His breath becoming howling, raging

116

wind, and terrible flashes of lightning, which was His own energy being torn from Him. He realized He had created a monster. He hurriedly built a fourth world so He could aim these lightning bolts at it to give a release valve for the pressure build-up on the third little world.

Michael watched, fascinated, as some of the strangest looking creatures began to develop on this fourth world, planet earth. They were fascinating and He watched as they grew larger and took many different forms and shapes. He wanted so badly to join them, to go down there and play with them. As the bolts of lightning kept getting larger and larger, that same thought kept coming back; "there has to be someplace else, something more than this. This is no good. We're just not getting anywhere at all here."

So one huge storm, the biggest on the whole of planet number three, the leader of the pack, you might say, formed into a lightning bolt very strong and determined to explore further as to what was out there. He gathered all His energy, took a huge breath, and exhaled, sending a very large lightning bolt over to planet four, earth. It was coming at a tremendous speed.

Thought-Form of Lucifer (Humanity) Moves to Earth

When this fourth world was completed the lightning coming from planet number three moved to it, along with the wind and rain. This large lightning bolt was the solar flare, Satania, from our sun Lucifer. At certain rhythmic periods these solar flares leave our sun Lucifer and are attracted to the planets in our solar system. These flares are not the Oversoul, remember. These flares are atmospheric disturbances in the form of storms, winds, tempest, etc. and are caused by the Oversoul. This was where the flare, Satania, was coming from, headed for planet earth. They came together.

Planet Earth

Earth, beautiful, verdant earth, that green jewel – and what's been going on with planet earth? What was going on with planet earth was the same thing that was going on with planet number three. Each of these planets remained the same as the previous planet until the thought forms, were ready to leave. Planet number one was air. When the thought form left planet number one it remained basically air even though it was separated into groupings on planet number two. When it left number two it was like graduation. It was not second plane dimension until it left number two. When it went from two to three it remained as second dimension until it worked it's way up through the processes on number three, and when it did, it graduated and left there as third dimensional consciousness and when it landed on planet number four it remained third dimensional consciousness.

You see, until we get through the life plan of this earth, we remain third dimensional consciousness until we graduate into fourth dimensional consciousness. There is an ethereal form around these planets which is where the true dimension of each planet is found. It's like a little cap up above it.

We are on the fourth planet, but most of humanity is still of third dimensional consciousness which is, remember, fighting, friction, hollering, hitting each other, murdering each other. All of that is still going on.

Stages of Progress

Michael, the Oversoul, began to go over in His mind the different stages of progress that He would like to see His children make. By this time He realized that eventually He was going to need another little world for them to progress to. He started to plan it and took into consideration what was going on down there in that world with all those different types pulling apart constantly. He realized that when they finally left planet earth after reaching the stage in evolution that He, as Oversoul had set for them, that they would need to be brought back together because, after all, they had started out as one and were shattered apart. No wonder they were lost and unhappy and fighting amongst themselves. What a shock to all, to be shattered into all those little sparks. No wonder they felt so alone, and they really and truly did need to help each other. But then, after all, He made that world as an experiment to be experienced in that way.

Put yourself into a "let's pretend" role of being the Oversoul. You know that when your children progress onward to the next stage of the path that you and your brothers laid out, they're going to need a period of healing before being shattered apart again for more lessons. After realizing that more worlds would be needed eventually, you and your brothers decide that you can cooperate and make a progressive path with the other worlds as advanced stages of that path.

Knowing that this group of yours is going to need at least one or two more worlds on which to be refined before they will be ready for the more advanced worlds of your brothers, you continue your work by creating the fifth world where they can recover and heal from the shock of life on the fourth planet. Even though they went through two stages or levels of life on the earth plane, they are nowhere near the level needed to join your brothers' worlds. The first stage of planet earth was third dimensional – being in manifestation (taking on a human form) – and the second was fourth dimensional, which is the unmanifested stage.

Even after the healing on the fifth world where the broken sparks are reunited, you feel they still need to have another experience in being separated, but this time as whole sparks again, not split into male and female halves. When they finish this experience they will finally be able to join those already on the seventh world. This seventh world is where the original help came from when you realized you needed to refine the early forms so the sparks could try again to enter them. Some of those who originally helped you are still on the seventh plane helping the newly arrived to adjust. Eventually they will move on. All keep moving along the path you and your brothers laid out.

The Oversoul is complete on planets one and two. He sends down his children (divine sparks) on planets three and four (earth), gathers them up on five to find out what they learned, sends them down on six and seven, gathers them up on eight, down again on nine and ten and up on eleven and twelve.

Remember, you created yourself from air that turned into rings of atoms that eventually started fighting and became storms and lightning. That lightning was your frustration of not being satisfied with what you thought was all of life. Look at the door that frustration opened for you. If you had never gotten frustrated enough to form lightning bolts that smashed into earth and shattered you, you would never have experienced all the different kingdoms inside yourself that you have so far experienced. There are more kingdoms yet to experience. You will always have more kingdoms ahead of you. As you keep expanding outward in your kingdoms, you will eventually return to your beginning and start all over again.

You begin to realize that reincarnation is the logical, sensible, compassionate way to run your little world. You realize you have done all you can as far as the seven different ray groups helping each other and you begin to see the necessity for rules and regulations to govern the cycle of lives. These rules and regulations would include the recirculation of these beautiful divine sparks of yours that really and truly try so hard at times to do the right thing, but still have many problems.

It will never stop. You will never stop being because you are a part of it all. There is no way you can get out of being part of the all. You are, and you may as well accept that there is so much more to you than you thought and accept that you are much more important than you thought, as you are God. You are the Creator God on all size scales!

Even though He sent off pieces of His energy in all directions, He kept them connected to Him by tiny threads. He would wait until He started receiving slight vibrations from one thread or another, then He would tune in to that communication line and feel what they were experiencing. He learned right from wrong by their experimentation. Then He would draw that thread back in and send it in a different direction to learn something else. That thread would be a certain length and every time it came back it would be a little shorter.

Eventually it would be too short to send out, so it would stay on with the whole of His being as a perfected part of Himself that would have to continue to learn through tuning into one of the communication lines that were still out there experiencing.

When all His lines or feelers had returned, He would be a pretty wise Oversoul, so He would be able to move on to the next classroom, the fifth planet, where He would not want to separate Himself. He would want to experience things as a whole soul, to keep all parts of Himself in a group and learn and experience in an enclosed situation, to synthesize what each individual thread experienced and determine what worked to make Him a better Oversoul and what didn't.

Oversouls

The term Oversoul has been overused. It should only apply to Oversoul Michael. But as there is a repeated pattern, it has been used as it dropped in octaves. Perhaps a numbering system could be instigated, much like our lineage – Oversoul senior, Oversoul junior, Oversoul I, Oversoul II, etc. This may be the best approach. There are seven octaves involved. You would get to Oversoul five if starting with senior and junior, or Oversoul seven if starting with Oversoul I.

Oversoul I - Michael (sometimes referred to as Christ Michael or Creator God Michael in the Chrysalis material) is Oversoul I.

Oversoul II - His twelve children are considered Level II Oversouls. The names of these are as follows: Lord Michael (sometimes referred to as Archangel Michael) the first born son. He was followed by Lord Raphael, Lord Maitreya, Lord El Terro, Lord Loren, Lord El Morya, Lord Darian, Lord Alfred, Lord Bater, Lord Norris, Lord Engleton, and Lord Phylon. They are better known as just "The Michael Sons." Some are well known, some are known not at all as they choose to not be. The Oversouls are, of course, related to divine evolution. Lucifer is related to physical evolution as Michael's physical sun, and along with the names of other planets – such as Phillipe for Sirion – must be considered the physical aura of the planets. Level II Oversouls are the spiritual auras and these are the names we wish to use. For example, El Terro is the esoteric aspect of earth and Lucifer the exoteric. In other words, El Terro is the "mind" of the planet and Lucifer the physical "form" or "body." As we are interested in the spiritual aspect we will use the spiritual terms as the Oversouls.

Oversoul III - The next level down is Oversoul Three. This is where you will find David (King David). There are only five, soon to be seven, on this level. They are the masters of the Ashrams on earth.

Oversoul IV - Oversoul four level is the seedcore level and there are no specific names given to these bodies.

Oversoul V - Oversoul five is the whole divine spark.

Oversoul VI - Oversoul six is the split spark.

Oversoul VII - Oversoul seven is the apex of our mind.

The Twelve Lords are the "passes through the Oversoul." Our planet has been through three passes and they are available to us now. The others will be in the future. The three we have passed through – the "three passes of the Oversoul" – have been El Morya, Raphael and Lord Maitreya. The new one coming up, the fourth pass will be El Terro for synchronizing with planet earth, the fourth planet. As some of the planets pass out of our galaxy their influence will be dropped off. This has happened with El Morya, and Raphael is fading out. Maitreya is very strong at the moment. It is his "turn" you might say, to direct the spiritual teachings on earth plane.

When El Terro becomes stronger, He will begin His teaching chores. These will be the restructuring concepts that are needed and necessary to follow on the heels of Maitreya's teachings. The two will serve together for a period of time, then Maitreya will begin fading and we will pick up the influence of Lord Loren. He is far out in space, but is next in line.

Lord Michael (Archangel Michael), the first born, is always available as a stepping stone to Oversoul Michael. Lord Michael is above the other spirit sons and touches and aids many other galaxies besides ours at all times. As the sons move out of our galaxy, they will enter another, or perhaps I should say as we move out of the influence of each son, another galaxy moves into that son's influence. This is the basis of astrology.

The Order of Melchizedek

The order of Melchizedek is a group which has formed a large conglomerate brotherhood that it is necessary to be through with earthly progression to belong to. It is a high teaching conglomerate stepping higher plane concepts down to the earth. There must be intermediaries between any of this order and any on the earth plane. They are what you could term Archangels in that they no longer descend anywhere near the earth plane. Their vibration is so high and refined that none on earth are capable of contact with them and let none tell you different. But they are extremely important to the direction of planetary life for all inhabited planets.

To Review

A comet from another galaxy had come to instigate the process of life in Michael the Oversoul, our Central Sun, to awaken Him and also our sun and its planets. The friction caused by this comet, the positive and negative subatomic particles, caused fiery gases to form and mix. Therefore, the spirit thought of the Creator is mixed with the fiery gases, the clouds, and the churning, boiling energy. So you see, even though Michael's spirit is still embedded in the Central Sun, this comet from outer space that originally came from the sixth universe, the one that awoke Michael to life, makes His orbit as the thought-form of Michael embedded in our Milky Way Galaxy.

This comet was made up of atoms from the first outer space level of the master universe, giving Michael His pool of genes, His atoms to use as He saw fit in the creation of His own universe. As an analogy, study the pollination process as carried on by insects in the Botanical Kingdom. It is the same exact process.

The first comet from outer space not only awoke Michael (gave birth to His mind), but also left His genes embedded in the sun and all the planets in our solar system that were forming and hardening. The way these genes were embedded was by being caught in the hardening and cooling process. They were caught in the form of suspended animation as the planets formed into solid bodies.

The central core of the universe is the Creator, the energy center. The flare that leaves the central universal core is the Oversoul. The sparks that shower from the Oversoul are our individual souls. It is like looking into a mirror, into a mirror, into a mirror, etc. This is how the universe seems and why it seems to have no boundaries and the pattern of creation is repeated over and over and over.

A comet is a thought-form of energy that leaves the central core and progresses through the universe and back. This comet of perfect, pure energy leaves the central core energy center on an exploration. It passes through black space near planets that are in a state of suspended animation (a solar system). The comet passes near enough to the first planet in the chain to stir the air into motion. This is the start of life and all proceeds through the first three planets forming the lightning bolt, (the Oversoul) which has twelve planets (planes) to progress through. This is one solar system (to us) but it is like one planet would be for the Oversoul. Our solar system is in the seventh universe in its chain which is the same as the seventh plane for the Oversoul. Then the Oversoul moves on to the next galaxy with twelve solar systems consisting of twelve planets each, which each have twelve planes. It progresses through twelve galaxies in this manner and returns to the starting point and begins the whole trip again.

126

The comets from the central core do not all follow the same path as far as which solar system they start in. They will follow the same path for that particular solar system, but may be totally different in looks (form) and still be much more evolved than us.

The central core sends the comet. This comet will make twelve trips through twelve planets, thereby having one hundred and forty-four probable realities. Each trip through, when it strikes earth, it sends out one hundred and forty-four tentacles that each divide into one hundred and forty-four sparks. These sparks split and each half spins off one hundred and forty-four probable realities, twelve reincarnations on each of the twelve levels.

You are a thought-form of energy, spun off that Oversoul, who progresses through twelve planes of inner life, which is mimicking the outer life (you), who is mimicking the Oversoul, who is mimicking the central core or God. You are the reality you at this given moment, and all others are the reality you on lower and higher levels. You can expand your universe by adding more mirrors to look into and extending your communication channel. Your soul is a child of the Oversoul, who is a child of the central core, the Creator, the same way your probable realities (other incarnations) are related to you.

Twelve Planes of Progress

The planets are in order as far as the progression of life upon them goes. The Oversoul's evolution is experienced on the physical bodies of the planets in our universe. Each solar system has or will have twelve planets for the Oversoul to progress through and each planet will have twelve planes for the thought-form (you) to progress through. We (humanity) are on the fourth planet, the third plane now. It takes a thought-form many thousands of years to progress past this plane. The next planet past earth is much different and very beautiful. The knowledge and teachings of these planets would be almost impossible to step down to any terminology that humanity could understand. It must be believed on faith that there is far to go.

From Michael

What a glorious, beautiful, fantastic place the earth is. I bless those with the courage to speak out in my behalf with the truth as it is encoded in their genes. It should not, cannot be the whole truth for others, but will help them decipher the truth for themselves.

130

Made in the USA
Las Vegas, NV
20 December 2023